OCCULT BOTANY

The Lore and Uses of Magical Plants

D.R. T STEPHENS

S.D.N Publishing

CONTENTS

GENERAL DISCLAIMER

This book is intended to provide informative and educational material on the subject matter covered. The author(s), publisher, and any affiliated parties make no representations or warranties with respect to the accuracy, applicability, completeness, or suitability of the contents herein and specifically disclaim any implied warranties of merchantability or fitness for a particular purpose.

The information contained in this book is for general information purposes only and is not intended to serve as legal, medical, financial, or any other form of professional advice. Readers should consult with appropriate professionals before making any decisions based on the information provided. Neither the author(s) nor the publisher shall be held responsible or liable for any loss, damage, injury, claim, or otherwise, whether direct or indirect, consequential, or incidental, that may occur as a result of applying or misinterpreting the information in this book.

This book may contain references to third-party websites, products, or services. Such references do not constitute an endorsement or recommendation, and the author(s) and publisher are not responsible for any outcomes related to these third-party references.

In no event shall the author(s), publisher, or any affiliated parties be liable for any direct, indirect, punitive, special, incidental, or other consequential damages arising directly or indirectly from any use of this material, which is provided "as is," and without warranties of any kind, express or implied.

By reading this book, you acknowledge and agree that you assume all risks and responsibilities concerning the applicability and consequences of the information provided. You also agree to indemnify, defend, and hold harmless the author(s), publisher, and any affiliated parties from any and all liabilities, claims, demands, actions, and causes of action whatsoever, whether or not foreseeable, that may arise from using or misusing the information contained in this book.

Although every effort has been made to ensure the accuracy of the information in this book as of the date of publication, the landscape of the subject matter covered is continuously evolving. Therefore, the author(s) and publisher expressly disclaim responsibility for any errors or omissions and reserve the right to update, alter, or revise the content without prior notice.

By continuing to read this book, you agree to be bound by the terms and conditions stated in this disclaimer. If you do not agree with these terms, it is your responsibility to discontinue use of this book immediately.

CHAPTER 1: THE GREEN MYSTERIES OF THE OCCULT

Introduction

Welcome to a verdant realm where the boundaries between the botanical world and the mystical overlap in fascinating ways. This chapter will serve as a threshold to the green mysteries, where we explore the occult aspects of plants, flowers, and trees. As you read on, consider this an invitation to deepen your understanding of how nature and the mystical intertwine, and how this union has been observed, celebrated, and utilized through ages.

The Symbiosis of Plants and Spirituality

Nature has been a sanctuary for spiritual exploration for millennia. Plants, in particular, have served a variety of roles in this context, far beyond their practical applications for food, shelter, and medicine. Throughout history, they have been imbued with symbolic meanings and magical properties, incorporated into rituals, and even believed to possess spirits or deities.

In various mythologies, trees are often seen as cosmic axis points linking heaven and earth, while herbs have been used in incantations and spells. The Druids in ancient Celtic traditions, for instance, viewed the oak tree as sacred and a symbol of the doorway between worlds. Similarly, in Vedic tradition, the soma plant was considered divine, and its juice was used in rituals to connect with the gods.

The Roots of Occult Botany

The term "occult" often evokes a sense of mystery or hidden knowledge, and when applied to botany, it refers to the arcane aspects of plant life. Ancient civilizations from Egypt to China to the Americas have their own systems of magical botany, where specific plants are used for divination, protection, and spiritual growth. These systems often feature in-depth lore that details the characteristics, harvesting methods, and ritual applications for each plant, creating a botanical lexicon that is as complex as it is enchanting.

The study of occult botany Is not limited to any one spiritual path. Whether you find your roots In Wicca, Shamanism, Kabbalah, or any other spiritual tradition, chances are you will find a rich history of plant use. Even monotheistic religions like Christianity have their own set of sacred plants, such as frankincense and myrrh, which were famously gifted to the infant Jesus according to biblical accounts.

Plant Symbolism and Metaphysical Properties

Plant symbolism permeates not only religious texts and mythological stories but also folklore and everyday customs. For example, the rose universally symbolizes love, while lavender often represents peace and tranquility. But these are not arbitrary associations. Plants also possess specific vibrational frequencies, which some believe interact with human energy fields.

In metaphysical terms, certain plants are believed to carry particular energies or correspondences. Sage, for example, is widely used for cleansing negative energy from spaces. The practice of "smudging" with sage has its origins in indigenous American traditions but has been adopted widely in various spiritual practices.

Furthermore, many herbalists and occult practitioners believe that plants have "spirits" or consciousness to some degree. In animistic traditions, plants are seen as allies, and working with plant spirits is considered a two-way relationship that requires respect and understanding.

Conclusion

Our exploration of the green mysteries is just beginning, but already we can see how deeply the realms of the botanical and the mystical are intertwined. This rich tapestry of beliefs, practices, and symbolism opens a path for anyone looking to deepen their spiritual practice with the aid of nature's bounty. Whether you are interested in the historical aspects, wish to incorporate more nature-based practices into your spiritual path, or are simply curious about the world of plants from an occult perspective, you are in for a nourishing journey.

As we venture further into specific plants, practices, and traditions in the following chapters, you'll find that the earth under your feet and the leaves over your head are teeming with magical potential, waiting to enrich your spiritual practice in ways you may never have imagined.

CHAPTER 2: THE HISTORICAL ROOTS OF MAGICAL PLANTS

Introduction

In this journey through the mystical world of plants, it's crucial to understand how deep the roots of plant-based magic go. History is rich with evidence that various cultures have integrated plants into their spiritual and magical practices. This chapter aims to take you on a voyage through time and space to explore how civilizations, from ancient to modern, have utilized the botanical world for occult purposes.

Mesopotamia and Ancient Egypt: The Cradle of Botanical Magic

Mesopotamia, often cited as the cradle of civilization, also holds significance for being one of the earliest societies to employ plants in their magical and medicinal practices. Ancient texts like the "Assyrian Herbal," a cuneiform script, provide references to the magical uses of plants such as myrtle and juniper for protection and purification. The relationship between humans and plants was considered sacred, woven into their myths like the Epic of Gilgamesh, which mentions the plant of immortality.

Likewise, Ancient Egypt was not far behind in recognizing the magical properties of plants. Plants like the blue lotus were symbolic of rebirth and transformation and were often depicted in frescoes and artifacts. Papyri from the New Kingdom period, such as the Ebers Papyrus, contain a myriad of prescriptions for herbal remedies that doubled as magical cures, providing a blend of medicine and magic that could ward off evil spirits or bring good fortune.

Greco-Roman Contributions: From Herbals to Lore

The Greco-Roman world carried the torch of botanical magic further. Works such as "De Materia Medica" by Pedanius Dioscorides offered comprehensive insights into the herbal lore of the time. Sacred groves dedicated to gods and goddesses like Athena and Demeter bore witness to the magical rites and rituals that often involved the use of specific plants like the laurel and olive. Moreover, Ancient Roman religious ceremonies like the Argei involved creating ritualistic effigies from reeds and rushes, reflecting the intrinsic link between the plant kingdom and spiritual practices.

Herbals, or books describing the properties of plants, became prevalent in the Roman period. These often combined scientific observations with folklore, yielding a rich tapestry of information that allowed for both medicinal and magical applications. The herbs discussed often carried a dual role, serving in healing practices and also as instruments for magical rites, such as using sage for wisdom and purification.

Medieval to Renaissance: The Alchemic Connection

As we move into the Medieval and Renaissance periods, alchemy and hermeticism took the historical stage, deeply influencing the way plants were perceived and used. The "Doctrine of Signatures," a belief that the physical attributes of plants could reveal their occult properties, was a popular concept during this time. Plants like the mandrake, with its human-like root, were imbued with magical attributes, often used in love spells and for protection.

Renowned figures such as Paracelsus were proponents of the magical uses of plants. Their writings contributed to the codification of plant magic, linking it explicitly with alchemical processes aimed at spiritual transformation. For example, the concept of the "Philosopher's Stone" was often linked with the perfection of both matter and spirit, and various plants were considered essential in this alchemical journey.

Modern Interpretations: Resurgence and Adaptations

In contemporary times, there has been a revival and adaptation of ancient practices. Neopagan movements like Wicca, and the broader umbrella of modern witchcraft, have embraced the lore and uses of magical plants, adapting ancient knowledge to modern contexts. The widespread availability of botanical knowledge, both through academic avenues and traditional wisdom, has democratized the use of plants in magical practices. New age spiritualism has also embraced the use of plant-based tools like smudge sticks, essential oils, and herbal talismans, proving that the roots of plant-based magic continue to grow and adapt.

Summary

Understanding the historical roots of magical plants provides invaluable context to their modern usage. From the ancient river valleys of Mesopotamia and Egypt to the philosophical circles of Greece and Rome, and through the mystical alchemists of the Medieval and Renaissance periods, the magical properties of plants have been acknowledged, documented, and employed in a myriad of ways. The thread of botanical magic weaves through the tapestry of human history, continually evolving but never breaking, reminding us of the enduring relationship between the plant kingdom and the realm of the mystical.

CHAPTER 3: PLANT SPIRITS AND ELEMENTAL BEINGS

Introduction

Welcome to this enchanting journey into the esoteric realms of plants. In this chapter, we delve into the complex metaphysical realm that intersects botany with spirituality: the notion of plant spirits and elemental beings. From the humblest herb to the most majestic oak, each plant is believed by many to possess a spirit or an essence that can interact with human consciousness.

The Concept of Plant Spirits in Different Traditions

In the rich tapestry of global spiritual traditions, the belief that plants have spirits or are animated by elemental forces is remarkably widespread. In shamanic practices, particularly among indigenous peoples in the Americas and Asia, the spirits of plants are considered vital allies. Shamans interact with these entities through rituals and altered states of consciousness, often gaining insights into healing or other forms of esoteric knowledge.

In Eastern traditions like Taoism and certain schools of Hinduism, plants are thought to be animated by "chi" or "prana," which are terms for life-force energy. Even the ancient Greeks had nymphs known as Dryads and Hamadryads that were believed to inhabit trees.

Western esoteric traditions, such as Hermeticism and the Kabbalah, also touch upon the spiritual essence of plants. In these traditions, the plant kingdom is associated with the elemental realm, with different plants corresponding to Earth, Air, Fire, and Water.

Elemental Beings and Plant Guardians

In some spiritual paradigms, plants are not just animated by a general life force but are believed to have specific guardians or elemental beings associated with them. Elemental beings—such as gnomes, sylphs, salamanders, and undines—are thought to be responsible for the nurturing and growth of plants. These elemental entities serve as intermediaries between the material and spiritual realms.

In Celtic and Nordic traditions, for instance, the spirits of the forest, often referred to as the "Fae" or "Hidden Folk," are intimately connected with the trees and plants in their domain. These beings are honored and appeased through various rituals to ensure the vitality of the flora as well as to gain their blessings or favor.

In many African and Afro-Caribbean spiritual practices, such as

Voodoo and Santeria, plants are seen as the abodes of spirits or "Orishas." These deities are often offered sacrifices and honored in rituals that involve the use of specific plants.

Engaging with Plant Spirits

How does one interact with plant spirits or elemental beings? The most common approach across traditions is through ritual and meditative practices. The aim is to shift one's consciousness to a level where interaction with these subtle entities becomes possible. Rituals often involve offerings, chants, and the use of talismans to attract the plant spirit or elemental being.

Another method is through "plant dieting," a practice common in South American shamanism where an individual abstains from certain foods and ingests small quantities of a particular plant over a period of time to align themselves with the spirit of the plant. This period of dieting is often accompanied by visions, dreams, and other mystical experiences that provide guidance or knowledge.

Some modern practices also involve the use of plant essences or flower remedies, like Bach Flower Remedies, to interact with the plant's spirit. These are dilutions of flower material developed in a way to capture its spiritual essence, which are then used for emotional and spiritual healing.

Summary

The realm of plant spirits and elemental beings opens a door into an intricate and spellbinding dimension where botany meets spirituality. Whether it's the shamans who enlist plant allies in their spiritual journeys, the Taoists who understand plants through the lens of life-force energy, or the Western magicians who engage with elemental beings, the idea that plants are imbued with spirit pervades many spiritual traditions. These beliefs invite us to consider plants not merely as biological entities but as spiritual companions, alive with a form of consciousness or spirit that we can interact with, learn from, and honor.

CHAPTER 4: THE DOCTRINE OF SIGNATURES

Introduction

The Doctrine of Signatures is a fascinating concept that has captivated the minds of herbalists, occultists, and natural philosophers for centuries. Rooted in the belief that the appearance of a plant—its color, shape, and texture—can give clues to its magical or medicinal properties, the doctrine offers a poetic lens through which to view the botanical world. Let's dive in and explore how this age-old wisdom still resonates today.

A Historic Overview

The concept of the Doctrine of Signatures can be traced back to ancient civilizations, but it gained significant prominence during the Renaissance. Paracelsus, a 16th-century Swiss physician and alchemist, was one of its most influential proponents. He argued that God had placed these 'signatures' or 'marks' on plants to indicate their utility. For Paracelsus, the idea was more than metaphorical; he firmly believed that the divine language was manifest in the natural world, and that understanding this language could aid in both magical and medicinal practices.

While Paracelsus is often credited with popularizing the Doctrine of Signatures, similar concepts existed in various cultures long before his time. The Greek physician Dioscorides, in his seminal work "De Materia Medica," hinted at the relationship between a plant's physical attributes and its potential uses, although he did not systematically organize these ideas into a formal doctrine. In traditional Chinese medicine and Ayurveda, similar principles were applied, associating the appearance or taste of plants with specific effects on the human body or spirit.

The Symbolic Language of Plants

When diving into the Doctrine of Signatures, it's crucial to approach it with a sense of wonder and humility, understanding that while not all modern scientific standards may validate the concept, it offers valuable insights into how our ancestors interacted with and understood the natural world. Let's consider a few illustrative examples:

- Heart-Shaped Leaves: Plants like the heart-leaved aster were traditionally believed to have an affinity with heart conditions. The similarity in shape between the plant's leaves and the human heart led herbalists to consider it a remedy for cardiovascular issues.

- Milk-Thistle: With its milky sap and liver-shaped leaves, milk-thistle has long been associated with liver health. Modern pharmacology has indeed confirmed the liver-protective qualities of this plant, particularly its active component, silymarin.

- Eyebright: This plant, with its tiny, bright flowers that resemble eyes, was used historically for various eye ailments. Although science may not fully confirm its efficacy for all eye conditions, eyebright does contain compounds known for anti-inflammatory properties.

The Doctrine in Contemporary Use

In the modern era, the Doctrine of Signatures is often viewed with a blend of scientific skepticism and poetic appreciation. While the idea that the physical appearance of a plant can dictate its utility has been largely debunked by scientific research, the doctrine remains a rich source of inspiration for herbalists and practitioners of plant-based magic. It serves as a framework that encourages a deeper, more intuitive relationship with plants.

Interestingly, current phytochemical research sometimes uncovers medicinal properties in plants that echo the traditional wisdom of the Doctrine of Signatures. For example, the antioxidants found in berries, often vibrant in color, have been scientifically shown to have protective effects on the human body, affirming the long-standing belief that colorful fruits hold life-affirming properties.

Summary

The Doctrine of Signatures is more than a quaint historical

concept; it is a window into the symbolic language of nature, inviting us to see plants as active participants in a grand, interconnected tapestry of life and wisdom. While the doctrine might not always stand up to rigorous scientific scrutiny, its lasting appeal attests to a human desire to find meaning and connection in the complexities of the natural world. So the next time you walk through a garden or a forest, take a moment to look closely. Who knows? Perhaps the plants are speaking to you in a language as old as time, waiting for you to decipher their secret signatures.

CHAPTER 5: HERBS OF THE WITCH

Introduction

Witchcraft, a term that encompasses a variety of pagan religious practices, has had a long-standing and intimate relationship with the botanical realm. This chapter dives deep into the green world of witchcraft, focusing on herbs that have been particularly prominent in these traditions. The chosen plants serve various roles, from aiding in rituals and spellwork to serving as tools for divination and protection.

The Triple Goddess: Maiden, Mother, Crone

A central theme in many witchcraft traditions, particularly in Wicca, is the worship of the Triple Goddess represented as the Maiden, Mother, and Crone. This tripartite view of femininity aligns well with the life cycle of many plants: from seed (Maiden), to full bloom (Mother), to wilting and seed production (Crone).

- Mugwort (Artemisia vulgaris): Traditionally associated with the Moon and the divine feminine, Mugwort has been used for its visionary properties. It is often used in divination and dream work, symbolizing the intuitive powers of the Maiden.

- Rosemary (Rosmarinus officinalis): This herb aligns with the Mother aspect, symbolizing fidelity, love, and memory. It is often used in love spells or rituals that call for nurturing energy.

- Sage (Salvia officinalis): Commonly used for cleansing and purification, sage is aligned with the Crone, the wise elder. This herb is most famously used in smudging ceremonies to cleanse spaces of negative energies.

The Four Elements: Earth, Water, Air, Fire

Another key aspect of witchcraft is the elemental framework, which categorizes natural phenomena into one of four elements —Earth, Water, Air, Fire. Various herbs are also classified based on their correspondences to these elements, each serving specific magical purposes.

- Earth (Patchouli - Pogostemon cablin): Patchouli has grounding properties and is commonly used in money and prosperity spells. The earthy aroma brings to mind the nurturing soil of the Earth, offering stability and foundation.

- Water (Chamomile - Matricaria chamomilla): Chamomile is linked to emotional healing and is often used in spells or rituals for peace, love, and tranquility. Its calming effects make it the perfect representative for the element of Water.

- Air (Lavender - Lavandula angustifolia): Often used for its calming and mental clarity-inducing properties, lavender aligns with the Air element. It is frequently used in spells that involve communication, travel, and intellectual pursuits.

- Fire (Cinnamon - Cinnamomum verum): Cinnamon is often used to add potency to spells and rituals. Its warming properties make it aptly associated with the Fire element, symbolizing transformation and change.

Practical Applications

So how do witches utilize these herbs? Generally, the herbs are incorporated into spell jars, sachets, or directly into ritual fires. They may be brewed into teas for consumption or ritual offerings. Infused oils using these herbs are often crafted for anointing or dressing candles. Dried herb bundles may also be created for smudging purposes. Importantly, many modern witches emphasize the use of ethically sourced or personally grown herbs to ensure that their practice is as sustainable as possible.

Each herb's magical attributes are most potent when the plant is harvested and prepared with intention. Timing is crucial; for instance, some traditions suggest harvesting during a specific moon phase or even at a particular time of day to maximize the plant's magical efficacy.

Conclusion

Witchcraft's relationship with the plant kingdom is ancient, rich, and deeply symbolic. By understanding the symbolic roles of specific herbs, you open up a wealth of magical possibilities for your own practice. Whether aligned with the Triple Goddess or connected to one of the four elemental energies, these herbs offer more than their mundane applications. They serve as powerful tools for change, insight, and spiritual enrichment. The key is to approach them with respect, ethical awareness, and a deep understanding of their traditional roles in the craft.

CHAPTER 6: SACRED TREES IN MYTHOLOGY AND MAGIC

Introduction

The majesty of trees has always captured human imagination. But beyond their observable grandeur lies a realm rich with symbolism and magic. This chapter takes you on an intriguing journey through the profound connections between trees and various mythologies, along with their significance in magical systems.

The Axis Mundi: Trees as Cosmic Connectors

One of the most potent archetypes related to trees is the concept of the Axis Mundi, or the "World Axis." This idea is prevalent in many cultures, and it portrays the tree as a cosmic pillar that connects the different realms of existence: Heaven, Earth, and the Underworld. The Norse Yggdrasil, the sacred ash tree, is an excellent example of this. Yggdrasil connects the Nine Worlds in Norse mythology, serving as a communication channel between gods, humans, and other creatures.

Similarly, in Hindu cosmology, the cosmic tree, or "Kalpavriksha," serves as the foundation of all existence, being born out of the primordial waters of creation. In Kabbalistic traditions, the Tree of Life, or "Etz Chaim," serves as a schematic representation of the universe and God's emanations. Here, the tree is less a physical entity and more a symbolic structure that helps practitioners understand complex spiritual concepts.

These trees are not mere plants but metaphysical entities that echo the interconnectedness of all life and spiritual realms. Their branches extend into the heavens, their trunks serve as the axis of the earthly realm, and their roots delve into the mysteries of the underworld. In ritualistic practices, invoking the image or concept of the Axis Mundi can help facilitate a spiritual connection between these realms, making trees indispensable in ceremonial magic.

Trees in Cultural Mythologies

Trees have also been central to various cultural mythologies, serving as symbols of life, wisdom, and power. In Celtic traditions, for instance, the oak tree is sacred and represents strength and endurance. It's frequently associated with the Druids, who are believed to have conducted religious ceremonies in oak groves. The Druids also revered the yew tree, which they saw as a symbol of death and rebirth, probably due to its long lifespan and the toxicity of its leaves and seeds.

In ancient Greek mythology, the olive tree was sacred to Athena, the goddess of wisdom. The tree came to symbolize peace and prosperity, and its oil was used in various religious and magical practices. The laurel tree, associated with Apollo, was considered a tree of inspiration and prophecy. Pythia, the high priestess at the Oracle of Delphi, is believed to have chewed laurel leaves to enter trances and offer prophetic insights.

In the African Yoruba tradition, the Iroko tree is considered sacred and is often linked with spirits and ancestors. The tree is thought to have magical properties, and rituals involving the Iroko often aim to invoke its spirit for blessings or guidance.

Magical Uses and Rituals

As potent symbols, trees have been incorporated into a multitude of magical practices. The wood from specific trees is often used to make wands, staffs, and ritual tools. For instance, willow wood is commonly used in moon magic and healing rituals, while hazel is favored for divination. In Druidic traditions, ogham staves, used for divination and alphabet magic, are often made from a variety of sacred trees including oak, ash, and thorn.

Tree leaves, bark, and resin are also commonly used in the making of incenses, oils, and talismans, each carrying their unique magical properties. For example, pine resin is often used for purification and protection spells, while the leaves of the bay tree are used for divination and to enhance psychic abilities.

In contemporary Wicca and neopagan practices, tree magic often involves meditative and visualization techniques. Practitioners might form a spiritual connection with a particular tree, absorbing its unique energy or even communicating with its spirit. This relationship can be nurtured over time, becoming a powerful aspect of one's magical practice.

Conclusion

Whether serving as cosmic connectors, cultural symbols, or active participants in magical rituals, trees have a multifaceted role in the world of occult botany. Their enduring symbolism across various cultures and mythologies attests to their universal appeal and spiritual potency. As we continue to explore the magical world of plants, the mystical allure of trees offers both deep wisdom and practical applications for our spiritual journey.

CHAPTER 7: ALCHEMIC BOTANY: PLANTS AND TRANSFORMATION

Introduction

As we delve deeper into the labyrinthine world of occult botany, let's shift our focus to a dimension where plants serve not just as magical tools but as agents of transformation—alchemic botany. In alchemy, plants are often used as raw materials for the Great Work, which is aimed at both the transformation of base metals into gold and the spiritual refinement of the self. This chapter illuminates how plants serve in alchemical processes, marking a nexus between the material and the spiritual.

Plants as Alchemic Symbols

In alchemical lore, plants are replete with symbolism. Just as metals like lead and gold correspond to specific stages in the alchemical process, plants too have their role in the narrative. For example, the Rose is a multifaceted symbol in alchemy often representing secrets, unfoldment, and even the Philosopher's Stone—the final goal of alchemy. In the hermetic arts, the Lily stands for purity and is often shown in conjunction with the Rose to symbolize the harmonization of opposites, a core alchemical theme.

Additionally, the process of plant growth itself is symbolic, mirroring the phases of alchemical work. The seed symbolizes the prima materia, or the first matter, from which all things come. The germination can be seen as the process of "nigredo" or blackening, a phase of decay and decomposition. This is followed by phases that correspond to growth, flowering, and finally fruiting, which align with subsequent stages of alchemy including "albedo" (whitening) and "rubedo" (reddening), culminating in the perfection of the matter at hand.

Plants in Spagyric Preparations

Spagyrics is a branch of herbal alchemy that focuses on the extraction and purification of plant essences for healing and spiritual illumination. The term 'Spagyric' comes from the Greek words "spaō," meaning "to draw out" or "to separate," and "ageirō," meaning "to gather" or "to combine." Essentially, spagyric preparations involve separating plant matter into its constituent parts—salt, sulfur, and mercury (not the actual elements but symbolic names for plant constituents)—purifying them, and then recombining them into a more potent form.

Common spagyric methods might include fermentation, distillation, and calcination. For example, the plant might be fermented to produce alcohol (the spirit or 'mercury'), then distilled to purify the essence ('sulfur'), and the remaining plant matter calcined to produce ash ('salt'). These are then recombined to produce a spagyric tincture or essence that not only serves medicinal purposes but is believed to have potent spiritual effects.

While spagyrics might sound arcane, many of these processes are rooted in genuine chemical reactions that alter the properties of the plant material. As such, some consider spagyrics to be a precursor to modern pharmacology, offering both practical and mystical insights into the nature of plants.

The Philosopher's Plant: Mandrake and Alchemy

No discussion of alchemic botany would be complete without mentioning the mysterious Mandrake (Mandragora spp.). Throughout history, Mandrake has been ascribed various magical and alchemical properties. It is said to be a key ingredient in making a homunculus—an artificial human—and its root, resembling a human figure, is believed to possess powers ranging from inducing love to facilitating astral projection.

The root of the Mandrake contains tropane alkaloids, which have powerful psychotropic effects. This chemical complexity makes it an ideal candidate for alchemical operations. However, due caution must be exercised due to the plant's toxic nature. It symbolizes the danger and promise of the alchemical path: potent transformative powers accompanied by significant risks, serving as a cautionary tale to those who tread this arcane avenue without adequate preparation.

Conclusion

Alchemy and botany share a long history, each illuminating different aspects of the other. Plants have served as both symbols and raw materials in alchemical processes, bridging the gap between the material and the spiritual. Whether through intricate symbolic associations or complex spagyric preparations, alchemy elevates the role of plants in magical practice to agents of profound transformation. As we transmute our understanding of plants from mere physical entities to potent spiritual allies, we are participating in our own version of the Great Work—the alchemical journey of soulful enrichment.

CHAPTER 8: FLOWER MAGIC: THE SUBTLE POWER OF BLOSSOMS

Introduction

Ah, flowers! Symbols of love, beauty, and ephemeral moments, they have captivated human senses since time immemorial. But beyond their aesthetic allure and fragrant offerings, flowers possess a cornucopia of magical properties. This chapter explores how the vibrant petals and subtle energies of blossoms have been harnessed for ritualistic and spiritual purposes.

Flowers as Symbols and Totems

One of the most fundamental ways in which flowers are used in magical practices is through symbolism. Different cultures and spiritual traditions associate specific meanings with particular flowers. For example, the lotus in Eastern traditions signifies purity and spiritual enlightenment, often depicted in the chakras as well as in Buddhist and Hindu iconography. In contrast, the rose is a complex symbol in Western esoteric traditions, representing divine love, secrecy, and wisdom, among other things.

Such symbolic uses aren't arbitrary but often find their roots in the innate characteristics of the flowers themselves. The lotus, for example, grows in murky waters but rises above the surface to bloom, which makes it an ideal representation of spiritual emergence. The rose, with its thorny stem and velvety petals, mirrors the duality of human experience—beauty and pain, love and sacrifice.

Flowers in Ritual and Spellwork

Flowers aren't just passive symbols; they are active magical ingredients in many spiritual practices. Whether fresh, dried, or as essential oils, flowers are a staple in spellwork, rituals, and even divination.

- Love Spells: Perhaps the most common use of flowers in magic is in love spells. Roses, being the ultimate symbol of love, are often used. Red roses are generally used to attract passionate love, while pink roses are for romantic love and white roses are for pure or spiritual love.

- Healing Rituals: Flowers like lavender and chamomile are employed in rituals aimed at healing or calming. These flowers have a dual role: their physical properties offer tangible health benefits, while their symbolic meanings further amplify the healing energies.

- Divination: Flowers like dandelions and calendulas have

been used in practices like "floromancy," a type of divination using flowers. For example, dandelion seeds are sometimes used to tell the direction or success of a venture based on the way they float in the air.

Incorporating flowers into your rituals usually involves placing them on altars, using them as offerings, or directly integrating them into spells. For instance, a flower may be carried as a talisman, brewed into a potion, or even used as a writing tool for inscribing symbols onto candles or paper.

Vibrational Essences: Flower Essences and Elixirs

Moving beyond the physical and symbolic uses, flowers are also used to create vibrational essences, such as flower essences and elixirs. Developed in the early 20th century by Dr. Edward Bach, flower essences capture the "life force" or "aura" of a flower in liquid form, usually water stabilized with a small amount of brandy. These essences are believed to carry the energetic imprint of the flower, and they can be ingested or applied topically to bring about emotional, mental, or spiritual change.

Flower essences are commonly used in holistic therapies today, often alongside other forms of natural healing like aromatherapy and crystal therapy. For example, the "Rescue Remedy" by Bach is a well-known flower essence combination designed to alleviate stress and anxiety. It's important to note that while flower essences are believed to work on an energetic level, scientific evidence supporting their efficacy is limited.

Summary

From time-honored symbolism to ritualistic applications and vibrational essences, flowers possess an array of uses in the realm of magical practices. They are not only beautiful decorations or simple gifts but also powerful tools for transformation, healing, and insight. As we admire their beauty, may we also remember their profound potential to touch the soul and influence the energies that animate our lives.

CHAPTER 9: ROOTS AND TUBERS: THE HIDDEN POWERS BENEATH

Introduction

While the beauty of flowers and the majesty of trees often take center stage in discussions about magical botany, roots and tubers hold a distinctive place in occult practices. Often concealed beneath the earth, they are akin to hidden treasures that possess potent magical properties. In this chapter, we delve into the mystical attributes of roots and tubers, the subterranean parts of plants that have been deeply embedded in various magical traditions.

Roots as Symbols of Foundation and Transformation

In magical symbolism, roots represent the foundational aspects of existence. They are where the plant connects with the Earth, drawing nutrients and providing stability. In many spiritual practices, roots are used to symbolize grounding and the anchoring of spiritual energy. For example, in Hoodoo and some

Western magical traditions, roots like mandrake and High John the Conqueror are carried as talismans for protection and to enhance one's foundational strength.

Roots are also integral to the idea of transformation. They are agents of change, transforming soil and water into nutrients for the plant. In alchemical symbolism, roots embody the transformative phase of "solve et coagula" — to dissolve and coagulate. In this regard, the use of roots in alchemical processes is an ancient practice that seeks to transmute base elements into higher forms. For example, the root of the Ashwagandha plant is frequently used in Ayurvedic medicine for its rejuvenating properties and is considered spiritually transformative.

Types of Roots and Tubers with Occult Significance

Different types of roots and tubers have varying magical properties, and their uses are quite diverse. Here are some particularly significant ones:

- Ginger Root: In Eastern and Western magical practices, ginger root is believed to speed up spells and rituals. It is often used in sachets, oils, and incenses to "heat up" the energy and promote quicker outcomes.

- Turmeric Root: Associated with purification and protection, turmeric is often used in rites and rituals aimed at clearing negative energies. It is a crucial element in Ayurvedic practices for both its medicinal and spiritual benefits.

- Calamus Root: Known for its association with control and domination spells, it's often used in Hoodoo to command respect or bend situations to one's favor.

- Dandelion Root: Commonly used in folk practices for divination and to enhance psychic abilities. It's also considered potent for spiritual cleansing.

- Yam and Sweet Potato: These tubers are rich in symbolism related to abundance and fertility. In various African and Native American traditions, they are used in rituals to invoke prosperity.

Practical Applications: Crafting Spells and Rituals

Using roots and tubers in magical work is a fascinating journey into the underbelly of the plant world. Many practitioners prefer to harvest their own roots, observing the lunar cycles and other astrological correspondences for maximum potency. However, if you're buying from a store or an online vendor, make sure they are ethically sourced.

For practical application, the roots can be ground into powders, turned into oils, or used whole in sachets and talismans. For example, a protective amulet can be crafted by filling a small bag with a mix of roots like turmeric for purification and High John for strength, then anointing the bag with a corresponding oil. For those interested in divination, a tea made of dandelion root can be consumed before engaging in practices like Tarot reading or rune casting to enhance psychic receptivity.

Roots and tubers can also be incorporated into candle magic. Carving your intention into a candle and rolling it in ground root amplifies the energy of your spell. Additionally, they can be used in the creation of magical inks, especially those intended for inscribing talismans or crafting spells requiring written words.

Conclusion

Roots and tubers provide an underexplored avenue into the rich tapestry of occult botany. Their qualities of grounding and transformation make them unique additions to a magical practitioner's toolkit. Whether used in talismans for protection, spells for transformation, or rituals for divination, these subterranean wonders offer a variety of magical uses that are as profound as they are practical. Next time you find yourself working on a spell or ritual, consider reaching below the surface—literally—to tap into the hidden powers that lie beneath the earth.

CHAPTER 10: HALLUCINOGENIC PLANTS AND SHAMANIC JOURNEYS

Introduction

For as long as humankind has existed, the pursuit of transcendent experiences has been a constant endeavor. While many cultures have discovered ways to glimpse beyond the veil of ordinary reality through fasting, meditation, and ritual, the plant kingdom has offered a unique pathway: hallucinogenic or entheogenic plants. In this chapter, we explore these unique botanicals and their significance in shamanic practices.

The Concept of Entheogens

The term "hallucinogenic" is often used interchangeably with "psychedelic" or "entheogenic," but they are not identical. Hallucinogens are substances that distort perception and thought processes. Psychedelics, a subset of hallucinogens, tend to induce experiences that are described as spiritual, or mystical. "Entheogen" is a term preferred in religious and spiritual contexts, derived from Greek words meaning "to generate the divine within." The plants under this category are not merely substances of leisure but sacred tools for spiritual awakening.

The idea of using plants for spiritual and divinatory practices is not new; it dates back millennia. Ancient Indian texts mention the use of Soma, a plant-based concoction, to connect with the divine. Similarly, the Eleusinian Mysteries in ancient Greece utilized a substance known as Kykeon, which is suspected to have had psychoactive properties. Shamanic traditions around the world often incorporate entheogenic plants to aid in journeying into the spirit realm or understanding the nature of existence.

Principal Entheogenic Plants and Their Uses

- Ayahuasca: A brew made from the Banisteriopsis caapi vine and various other plant ingredients, commonly used in the Amazon basin. It's often consumed in a ceremonial context under the guidance of a shaman. Ayahuasca is known for its profound spiritual and psychological effects.

- Peyote: A small cactus native to the southwestern United States and Mexico, containing mescaline, a potent psychoactive alkaloid. It is used primarily by Native American communities in religious ceremonies.

- Psilocybin Mushrooms: Commonly referred to as "magic mushrooms," these fungi contain the psychoactive compounds psilocybin and psilocin. They are used in various indigenous cultures and modern spiritual practices for their introspective and mystical effects.

- Cannabis: Though not often considered in the same league as the other entheogens, Cannabis has been used in spiritual contexts in Hinduism (as bhang), Rastafarianism, and other religious practices.

- Iboga: Native to West Africa, this plant is rich in the alkaloid ibogaine and is a central part of the Bwiti religion. It's reputed for its intense, life-altering experiences and is sometimes used to treat addiction in a ritual context.

Ethical and Safety Concerns

While entheogenic plants hold immense potential for spiritual growth, they also come with a set of ethical and safety considerations. The consumption of such plants should be approached with respect, adequate preparation, and preferably, under the guidance of a knowledgeable guide or shaman. The setting or 'set and setting' in which these substances are consumed is of the utmost importance. Often, traditional shamanic practices involve specific preparatory phases, including fasting and other purification rituals.

Moreover, the rise in "spiritual tourism," particularly related to Ayahuasca, has led to concerns about the exploitation of indigenous knowledge and the sustainability of these plants.

Ethical sourcing and a respect for the traditions from which these plants originate are critical elements in responsible entheogenic practices.

Conclusion

The world of entheogenic plants offers a window into dimensions of consciousness that are as profound as they are mysterious. Whether seen as sacraments, medicines, or teachers, these plants have been integral to the spiritual practices of various cultures for millennia. However, their power demands respect, and their use requires preparation, caution, and, ideally, guidance. As more people turn to these ancient botanical pathways in search of spiritual enlightenment, it remains crucial to approach them with the reverence they have commanded throughout history.

CHAPTER 11:
POISONOUS PLANTS
IN OCCULT PRACTICES

Introduction

Welcome to a chapter that demands particular care and attention —poisonous plants in occult practices. These plants possess an allure that is both captivating and dangerous. The power they hold is profound but comes with ethical considerations and risks that require mature handling. We will delve into the historical uses, the symbolism, and the practical and ethical considerations surrounding toxic plants in magic.

The Historical Allure and Symbolism

The use of poisonous plants dates back to ancient civilizations. The Greeks were well-acquainted with the dangerous effects of aconite and belladonna, while the Egyptians recorded the effects of plants like henbane. Often, these plants were linked to gods and goddesses of death and the underworld, symbolizing the transformative power of life and death, change, and rebirth.

In medieval European witchcraft, the use of "baneful herbs"—

herbs that can cause harm, sickness, or death—were often associated with witches' ointments and flying potions. Plants like belladonna, mandrake, and henbane were said to be used in rituals and spells that sought transformation or communion with other realms. In the Celtic tradition, yew trees, which are toxic to humans and animals, are considered gateways to the otherworld and are often found in sacred burial grounds.

Symbolically, poisonous plants often represent the darker aspects of life: death, the underworld, transformation, and even hidden wisdom. They are the botanical expressions of the mysteries that many fear to tread. In certain esoteric traditions, working with these plants is a rite of passage that signifies mastery over life and death.

Practical Uses in Rituals and Magic

Using poisonous plants in magic is not for the faint-hearted or the inexperienced. Extreme caution is required, along with a deep understanding of the plant's toxicology. The following are some ways in which poisonous plants are traditionally used in magical practices:

- Protection Spells: Plants like aconite and hellebore have historically been used to guard against negative energies or malevolent entities.

- Divination: Certain poisonous plants like wormwood, when used cautiously, can be incorporated into ointments or incenses that aid in divinatory practices.

- Spirit Communication: The toxicity levels of plants like belladonna and datura have been minimized through various preparations to facilitate communication with spirits or deities.

Before you even consider incorporating a poisonous plant into your ritual, research thoroughly about its toxicity levels, preparation methods, and antidotes. Consult with experts in both botany and occult practices. The margin for error is exceedingly thin, and the consequences can be fatal.

Ethical and Safety Considerations

Working with poisonous plants in magical practices raises inevitable ethical concerns. Here are a few points to consider:

- Consent: If your practice involves others, their informed consent is crucial. They should be aware of the risks involved and willingly participate.

- Legal Restrictions: Some poisonous plants are also controlled substances. Make sure to understand the laws in your jurisdiction about the possession and use of such plants.

- Sustainability: If you're sourcing these plants from the

wild, it's vital to do so sustainably. Many toxic plants are also endangered and protected by laws.

- Animal Safety: Make sure that the plants you use are kept out of reach of pets and other animals.

- Disposal: Be careful in disposing of plant matter. The ecological impact could be significant if these plants are not disposed of properly.

Lastly, but most importantly, ethical magical practice demands respect for all life forms, including plants. These powerful botanicals are not mere tools to be exploited but are beings with their own intrinsic value and should be approached with the utmost reverence and care.

Summary

The realm of poisonous plants in occult practices is both tantalizing and perilous. While they offer potent energies for transformative magical work, they demand respect, comprehensive knowledge, and ethical integrity. Tread carefully in this arcane botanical field; the rewards are immense, but the penalties for carelessness can be severe. Always prioritize safety, ethics, and legality when dealing with these baneful herbs. After all, wisdom is the greatest magical tool you possess.

CHAPTER 12: INCENSE AND RESINS: SMOKE OF THE SPIRITS

Introduction

We've explored the magical uses of various types of plants, from poisonous herbs to fragrant flowers. Now let's delve into another fascinating facet of botanical mysticism: the use of plants in creating incense and resins for spiritual and magical applications. The burning of incense has been a practice interwoven with human spirituality for thousands of years, and the role of plants in this ritual is indispensable.

The History and Symbolism of Incense in Spiritual Practices

The practice of burning incense is not limited to one cultural or religious context. It spans various traditions including Hinduism, Buddhism, Christianity, and indigenous religions, to name a few. The word 'incense' itself comes from the Latin 'incendere,' meaning 'to burn,' and the act of burning these aromatic substances has been widely seen as a means to purify an area, to act as an offering to the divine, or even to serve as a vehicle for prayer.

Most of these practices involve the use of plant-derived materials. Herbs, tree resins, and flowers are often turned into incense either by direct burning or by being processed into sticks or cones. Frankincense and myrrh, perhaps the most iconic of all incense resins, are both derived from tree sap and have been used since ancient times in religious ceremonies.

The symbolic connotations of incense vary from one tradition to another. In some Christian rites, for instance, incense symbolizes the prayers of the faithful rising to heaven. In Eastern practices like Taoism and Shingon Buddhism, the aroma of incense is believed to purify the mind and surroundings, promoting meditative focus and spiritual clarity.

Types of Plant-Based Incenses and Resins

There is a remarkable diversity in the kinds of plant materials used to produce incense. Here are some notable examples:

- Frankincense: Derived from the resin of the Boswellia tree, frankincense is one of the oldest and most revered types of incense. It is commonly used for purification and deepening meditative states.

- Myrrh: Like frankincense, myrrh is also a resin, obtained from the Commiphora species of trees. It is often used for spiritual protection and cleansing.

- Sandalwood: Obtained from the heartwood of the sandalwood tree, sandalwood incense has a rich, woody aroma and is widely used in Hindu and Buddhist rituals for promoting mental clarity.

- Lavender: Known for its calming effects, lavender incense is often used in practices aimed at relaxation or stress relief.

- Sage: Popular especially in Native American smudging ceremonies, dried sage is believed to have powerful cleansing properties.

Practical and Ethical Considerations

When using incense and resins in your spiritual or magical practices, there are some crucial considerations to bear in mind. First, it's essential to ensure that the plant materials you're using have been sustainably sourced. Overharvesting of plants like frankincense and sandalwood has put significant strains on these species. Ethical sourcing ensures that we can continue to use these remarkable substances without endangering their survival.

Secondly, consider the health implications. Some people are sensitive to smoke, so be sure to use incense in a well-ventilated area and take precautions if you know you have respiratory issues. The practice should enhance your spiritual journey, not jeopardize your well-being.

Conclusion

The use of plant-derived incense and resins is a practice deeply entrenched in human spiritual history. From the ancient rituals involving frankincense and myrrh to modern-day meditative practices with lavender and sandalwood, these substances continue to offer a multi-sensory enhancement to our spiritual experiences. Whether used for purification, as an offering, or a facilitator for prayer and meditation, the botanical origins of these powerful substances serve to deepen our connection to the earth even as they elevate our spirits. By making ethical choices in sourcing and using these materials, we honor both the plants and the traditions they enrich.

CHAPTER 13: FRUITS OF FATE AND FORTUNE

Introduction

We've journeyed through the roots, leaves, and blossoms of the magical botanical world. Today, let's explore an often overlooked but equally potent aspect: fruits. Brimming with the culmination of a plant's life cycle, fruits carry within them the essence of the plant's energy, and by extension, its mystical properties. In this chapter, we shall delve into the intricate connections between fruits and various magical traditions, their symbolism in folklore, and their practical applications in contemporary spiritual practices.

The Symbolism of Fruits In Mythology and Folklore

Throughout history, fruits have been laden with symbolic meaning, often representing abundance, fertility, and transformation. Their cyclical nature—from seed to fruit-bearing maturity and back to seed—links them inherently with themes of life, death, and rebirth. In Greek mythology, for instance, the pomegranate is linked to the tale of Persephone, whose consumption of its seeds ties her to the Underworld for part of each year. This has resulted in the pomegranate becoming a symbol of cycles, commitments, and the mystical divide between different realms of existence.

Apples have also played a significant role in Western folklore and myth. The apple appears as a symbol of knowledge, temptation, and transformation in Biblical stories, and in the lore of the Celts, apples were considered the fruit of the gods and a symbol of eternal life. This symbolism extends to magical traditions where apples are often used in divination and love spells.

In Eastern philosophies like Hinduism and Buddhism, fruits like the fig and the mango hold sacred significance. The fig, particularly the species Ficus religiosa, under which Buddha is said to have achieved enlightenment, is viewed as a symbol of spiritual awakening. The mango is often associated with love and fertility and is even sometimes symbolized as the cosmic egg in Hindu cosmology.

Mystical Applications of Fruits in Rituals and Magic

Beyond their symbolic implications, fruits have been directly incorporated into magical practices for centuries. They act as talismans, offerings, or ingredients in spellwork, and they contribute their unique vibrational energies to enhance magical outcomes.

For instance, oranges and lemons are often used in spells and rituals aimed at bringing joy and positivity. Their bright colors and uplifting scents naturally align with these intentions. The juice, peel, and even the leaves of the tree can be utilized in various forms—be it sachets, incense, or anointments.

Berries, particularly blackberries and blueberries, have been traditionally used for protection spells. Their dark color is often associated with absorbing or repelling negative energies. Incorporating berries into your protective amulets or even just placing a bowl of them near an entryway can serve as a practical approach to safeguard your space.

Ethical Considerations: Harvesting and Consumption

While the use of fruits in magical practices holds immense potential, it also demands ethical considerations. Just like with any other plant materials, responsible and sustainable harvesting is crucial. Be conscious of where your fruits are coming from, especially if they are being gathered in the wild. Make sure not to deplete natural resources and to leave enough for wildlife and natural propagation.

For fruits that are grown using industrial agricultural methods, consider the implications of pesticides and ecological impact. Whenever possible, opt for organically grown produce or, better yet, try growing your own magical fruit garden to ensure that the energies are pure and attuned to your intentions.

Conclusion

Fruits, in their luscious and varied forms, offer not just nutritional sustenance but also rich symbolic meanings and mystical powers. Their cyclical growth patterns connect them to life's grand cycles, and their rich mythological associations weave them into the tapestry of humanity's spiritual narrative. Through understanding these layers, we can utilize fruits as powerful instruments in our magical practices, for everything from protection to prosperity. Like the magical plants discussed in previous chapters, fruits offer yet another door into the interconnected mystery of the natural world and its spiritual dimensions. Through them, we can tap into ancient wisdom while adding a layer of richness to our contemporary spiritual practices.

CHAPTER 14: THE BOTANY OF VOODOO AND HOODOO

Introduction

In this journey through the mystical world of plants, we've traversed various cultures and spiritual traditions to understand how flora intersects with the arcane. Now, we dive into the rich, complex, and often misunderstood traditions of Voodoo and Hoodoo to explore their unique relationship with plants. Through the lens of Afro-Caribbean spirituality, we will delve into the botanical aspects that form the backbone of many rites, spells, and rituals.

Essential Plants in Voodoo and Hoodoo

The rituals in Voodoo and Hoodoo are deeply rooted in the use of botanical elements. In both traditions, plants serve as potent tools for healing, protection, and transformation. It's important to clarify that Voodoo is a religion with roots in West African Vodun, while Hoodoo is a system of magical practices that developed among African Americans in the U.S. Although they share some similarities, they are not the same.

One of the most iconic plants associated with Voodoo and Hoodoo is the High John the Conqueror root (Ipomoea jalapa). This root is said to bring strength, luck, and personal mastery. In Hoodoo, it is often carried as an amulet or used in rootwork for various spells. High John the Conqueror root has a rich history that is intertwined with tales of a folk hero who embodies resilience and ingenuity.

Mugwort (Artemisia vulgaris) is another plant that holds a special place in these traditions. It is considered protective and is often used in dream-related work. Mugwort can be placed under a pillow to induce prophetic dreams or burned as incense during divination.

Similarly, Vervain (Verbena officinalis) is highly regarded for its magical properties. Known for its abilities to offer protection against evil spirits and to enhance various other spells, vervain is a multifaceted herb in Afro-Caribbean magical practices.

The Ethnobotanical Angle

It is fascinating to explore these traditions from an ethnobotanical perspective, understanding how native plants of West Africa, for example, have been replaced or supplemented by New World flora. The merging of Old and New World plants in the diaspora has created a rich tapestry of botanical lore. Certain African plants that were not available in the Americas had their roles assumed by local or naturalized plants. This is a vivid example of how belief systems adapt and evolve when transferred to new geographical and cultural contexts.

For instance, the Calabar bean, native to West Africa, was employed in oracular and judicial practices in its homeland. Once transported to the New World, its role was often assumed by the indigenous Datura plant, known for its powerful, mind-altering properties.

Ethical Considerations

While the study of the botanical aspects of Voodoo and Hoodoo is undeniably fascinating, it is crucial to approach it with cultural sensitivity and respect. These are living traditions practiced by people who have often faced marginalization. Ethical considerations extend to the plants as well. Overharvesting of certain species for magical or commercial use poses a significant ecological concern. As with all magical practices involving botanical elements, sustainable and respectful gathering methods should be employed.

Conclusion

The plant lore of Voodoo and Hoodoo is a rich, intricate facet of these complex spiritual systems. From the legendary High John the Conqueror root to the protective virtues of mugwort and vervain, each plant holds a narrative deeply ingrained in the cultural fabric of these traditions. Even more fascinating is the adaptive nature of these practices, wherein the unavailability of specific plants led to a syncretic fusion of Old and New World botany.

As you explore the magical properties of these plants, remember to approach both the botany and the cultural aspects with the respect and reverence they deserve. Whether you're a practitioner or a scholar, understanding the role of plants in Voodoo and Hoodoo enriches not only our comprehension of these specific traditions but also our broader appreciation for the mystical potential of the plant kingdom.

CHAPTER 15:
AYURVEDIC PLANTS
AND EASTERN
MYSTICISM

Introduction

Eastern mysticism, with Ayurveda as one of its most revered branches, offers a fascinating realm where plants are not just elements of nature but integral components of spiritual, mental, and physical well-being. Ayurveda, which translates to "the science of life," is rooted in the belief that balance and harmony between the energies within and around us lead to wellness. In this chapter, we will journey through the landscape of Ayurvedic botany and explore how it intersects with Eastern spiritual traditions.

The Three Doshas and Plant Correspondence

In Ayurvedic philosophy, the concept of the 'Doshas' plays a central role. These are three bodily humors—Vata, Pitta, and Kapha—that govern physical and mental processes. The Doshas are dynamic energies derived from the five elements: ether, air, fire, water, and earth. Plants, too, are categorized according to these Doshas, based on their properties.

- Vata (Air & Ether): Plants that are warm, oily, and heavy are considered beneficial for balancing Vata. Ginger, for instance, is warm and anti-inflammatory, making it a go-to for countering the dry, cold attributes of Vata imbalance.

- Pitta (Fire & Water): Cooling, calming plants like mint or aloe vera are Pitta-balancing. These plants help in reducing inflammation and heat in the body.

- Kapha (Water & Earth): Stimulating and heating plants such as pepper or garlic are beneficial for balancing Kapha. They help in reducing sluggishness and excess moisture.

When practitioners choose plants for medicinal or ritualistic use, these Dosha-balancing attributes often come into play. They are essential in defining how a particular plant will interact with the individual's unique constitution.

Plants in Ayurvedic Rituals and Spirituality

Ayurvedic practices are inherently spiritual, often blurring the lines between what we consider 'medicine' and what we regard as 'ritual.' Some plants hold particular significance in both these contexts:

- Tulsi (Holy Basil): This plant is venerated and often grown in household yards in India. It's believed to be an earthly manifestation of the goddess Lakshmi. Tulsi leaves are not just a regular feature in Ayurvedic medicine but also a crucial part of rituals and prayers.

- Neem: Traditionally used for its antibacterial and antiviral properties, Neem is also associated with the goddess of smallpox, Shitala. Special rituals involving Neem are performed to seek her blessings for protection against diseases.

- Bhringraj: Known as the 'king of hair,' this plant is widely used for promoting hair growth. Spiritually, it's associated with the lord of the celestial physicians, Dhanvantari, and is often used in rituals seeking health and vitality.

The spiritual and medicinal applications are so interwoven that it's often hard to separate the two. Many practitioners of Ayurveda also participate in traditional ceremonies that invoke deities or energies related to specific plants.

Interconnectedness of Ayurveda and Yoga

The harmonizing principles of Ayurveda find resonance in another spiritual practice: Yoga. Yoga postures, breath control techniques, and meditative practices often accompany Ayurvedic therapies to enhance their efficacy. Plants like Ashwagandha, known for its adaptogenic properties, are often recommended to Yogis for increasing stamina and reducing stress. The synchronization of Yoga and Ayurveda presents a holistic approach where plants play a critical role in nurturing the body, mind, and spirit.

Conclusion

Ayurvedic botany offers a lens through which we can explore the profound connections between the plant kingdom and human well-being. Whether it is balancing Doshas or engaging in spiritual rituals, plants in Ayurveda serve as powerful agents for transformation and harmony. They're more than mere components in a prescription; they are sacred entities that interact with us on an elemental level. Thus, the journey into the world of Ayurvedic plants is, in essence, a journey into the heart of Eastern mysticism itself.

CHAPTER 16: THE PLANT KINGDOM AND QABALAH

Introduction

The Kabbalistic Tree of Life has captivated the minds of mystics, scholars, and spiritual seekers for centuries. It's a diagrammatic representation that is often used to understand the nature of the Divine, the cosmos, and the human psyche. But how does the Tree of Life intersect with the botanical world? This chapter aims to explore the compelling connections between the Kabbalistic Tree of Life and the plant kingdom, enriching our understanding of how the natural and spiritual worlds intertwine.

The Tree of Life and Its Spheres

The Kabbalistic Tree of Life consists of ten spheres, known as "Sephiroth," connected by twenty-two pathways. Each sphere represents an aspect of the Divine, an emanation through which the ineffable manifests. While the Sephiroth themselves are often discussed in abstract terms, various traditions have associated them with more tangible elements, such as planets, animals, and even plants.

For instance, the first sphere, "Keter" or "Crown," embodies pure consciousness, the source of all creation. In the realm of plants, this could be akin to the primal energy of life that resides in every seed. It is the spark of potential, the essence from which all plants spring forth. The following spheres, like "Chokhmah" (Wisdom) and "Binah" (Understanding), could be related to the branching out and the roots, representing the expansion and limitations that are part of every life form.

Sephirotic Plants and Their Attributes

Each Sephira on the Tree of Life is associated with various plants whose characteristics symbolize the qualities of that particular sphere. Let's consider a few examples:

- Malkuth (Kingdom): Representing the material world, Malkuth can be symbolized by plants that are grounded and practical in their uses. Think of the common herbs like sage, used both for culinary and cleansing rituals, or the robust oak tree, a symbol of strength and endurance.

- Tiferet (Beauty): This Sephira embodies harmony and compassion, represented by plants like lavender or rose. These are plants often used in healing and peace rituals, their aesthetic and aromatic qualities symbolizing balance and beauty.

- Gevurah (Judgment/Strength): This sphere of restraint is symbolized by plants like nettle or thistle, plants that offer benefits but demand respect due to their prickly or stinging nature.

While these correspondences can serve as a guide, remember that the beauty of spiritual practice lies in personal interpretation and intuition. You may find other plants that, for you, better capture the essence of a particular Sephira.

Practical Applications in Ritual and Meditation

The idea of associating plants with the Sephiroth can be incorporated into your spiritual practice in various ways. You might create a Tree of Life altar featuring the corresponding plants, or incorporate these plants into rituals aimed at invoking the energies of specific Sephiroth. During meditation, visualize the Sephiroth and their associated plants as a means of drawing down the energies you seek to embody.

In addition, you can cultivate these Sephirotic plants in your magical garden, working to instill their specific energies into your surroundings. The act of planting, tending, and harvesting them can become a ritual in itself, mirroring the mystical concepts they represent.

Conclusion

The intersection of the Tree of Life with the botanical realm offers us a rich tapestry of symbolism and practical spirituality. By associating particular plants with the Sephiroth, we give ourselves tactile, living points of connection to higher spiritual truths. It's a fascinating journey of exploring how each plant embodies divine principles, serving as both metaphor and material in our ongoing spiritual journey. Whether used in meditation, ritual, or simple reflection, these associations can enrich our understanding of both the natural world and the ineffable mysteries of the divine.

CHAPTER 17:
NORDIC AND CELTIC
PLANT LORE

Introduction

The expansive green landscapes of the Celtic and Nordic regions have provided a rich tapestry for a myriad of mystical practices, rituals, and beliefs. Central to these are the local plants, trees, and herbs that have been deeply enmeshed in both the mythologies and magical practices of these cultures. Let's journey through the rich botanic world of the Celtic and Nordic traditions, and explore the magical significance of the local flora in these age-old systems.

Plants in Nordic Mythology and Magic

The botany of the Nordic regions, characterized by a mixture of deciduous and evergreen forests, has been of critical importance in Scandinavian mythology and magical practices. The Yggdrasil, or the World Tree, for example, is a central cosmological figure that links the nine worlds in Norse mythology. Often represented as an ash tree, Yggdrasil stands as a symbol of the interconnectedness of all realms of existence.

The ash tree itself has been considered sacred and is believed to have protective qualities. In runic alphabets, the ash is associated with the rune named "Ansuz," which represents the Aesir gods, primarily Odin, and is believed to bring about effective communication and wisdom. It's not uncommon for traditional Nordic practitioners to carry ash wood talismans or use ash leaves in their spells and rituals.

Juniper and rowan trees also feature prominently in Nordic magic. Juniper's protective properties are often utilized in charms and amulets, while rowan, linked to the rune "Raidho," has been used for both journeying and protection against malevolent spirits.

The use of plants for "seidr," a form of Nordic shamanic practice, involved diverse plant species, including mugwort. Mugwort is an herb often used to aid in divination and to bring about prophetic dreams. It was likely used in seidr for journeying through the realms or communicating with the spirit world.

Plants in Celtic Mythology and Magic

The Celtic tradition, spread across regions including present-day Ireland, Scotland, and Wales, also boasts a rich plant lore. The oak, ash, and thorn often appear together in Celtic myth and are believed to mark the entrance to the Otherworld when found growing together. The oak tree, sacred to the Druids, symbolizes strength and endurance and is associated with the god Dagda.

One of the most celebrated plants in the Celtic world is mistletoe. Known in folklore for its healing and fertility attributes, mistletoe was also considered a plant of protection against evil spirits. Druids are often depicted harvesting mistletoe with a golden sickle, highlighting the plant's significance.

Gorse, heather, and elder are also significant in Celtic plant magic. Gorse is used for protection and money-drawing spells, while heather is often used in rituals to enhance spiritual development and to honor the dead. Elder, on the other hand, is somewhat dual-natured. Its berries are often used in protective charms, but the elder tree is also regarded with a sense of caution, as it's believed to be inhabited by the Elder Mother, a spirit who could either bless or curse those who encounter her.

Bridging Traditions: Shared Themes and Modern Practices

While the Nordic and Celtic traditions hail from different regions and historical contexts, they share several themes, such as the reverence for trees and the use of plants for protection, divination, and spiritual journeys. Modern practitioners who draw inspiration from these traditions often find that the magical properties attributed to these plants are consistent with the broader magical correspondences found in the Western esoteric tradition.

In today's magical practices, it's common to see individuals combining elements from both Nordic and Celtic plant lore in their spells, rituals, and charms. For example, one might use both ash wood and oak in a protective talisman, invoking both the power of the Yggdrasil and the strength of the Dagda. Through thoughtful integration, these rich traditions offer an expansive herbal toolkit for contemporary magical practice.

Conclusion

The plants and trees of the Nordic and Celtic regions are deeply interwoven with the mythologies, spiritual beliefs, and magical practices of these areas. Whether it's the towering ash tree connecting the realms in Norse cosmology or the sacred oak central to Celtic Druidic practices, the flora in these traditions serve not merely as passive backdrops but as active participants in the sacred stories and rituals of these cultures. Even in modern times, the knowledge of these plants and their magical properties continues to enrich and deepen the practices of those who feel called to explore the green mysteries of the North.

CHAPTER 18: AMAZONIAN PLANT MAGIC

Introduction

Journeying to the heart of the Amazon Rainforest, we uncover the botanical treasures that have been an integral part of indigenous cultures for generations. This chapter aims to delve into the mystical uses of Amazonian plants, connecting ancient wisdom with modern understanding. With a focus on the spiritual significance, we explore the relationships between people and plants in one of the most biodiverse ecosystems on Earth.

Amazonian Spiritual Ecology

The indigenous communities of the Amazon have a complex spiritual ecology that ties them to their environment in intricate ways. Unlike more materialistic or reductionist viewpoints, Amazonian tribes view plants not just as resources but as beings with spirits, wisdom, and intentions. For example, the Shipibo people of Peru are known for their intimate relationship with Ayahuasca, a psychoactive brew made from the Banisteriopsis caapi vine and the leaves of the Psychotria viridis. This brew is central to their cosmology, used to connect with the spirit world and gain insight into healing and wisdom.

Another aspect is the concept of "plant teachers," revered plants that offer not just material benefits but spiritual lessons. These include plants like the tobacco (Nicotiana rustica), which is viewed as a potent spiritual ally rather than just a smokable substance. It's often used in small amounts to induce visionary states and is considered a medium for communication with the spirit world.

Magical Uses of Amazonian Plants

- Ayahuasca: Known scientifically as Banisteriopsis caapi, this vine is often combined with other plants to create a brew with psychoactive properties. Shamans use this mixture to gain insights into illness, emotional suffering, or spiritual quests. The visions induced by Ayahuasca are considered messages from the spirit realm.

- Guayusa (Ilex guayusa): Indigenous communities in Ecuador use the leaves of this holly tree for divination and dream interpretation. It is commonly consumed as a tea to help keep shamans awake during nighttime ceremonies.

- Sangre de Drago (Croton lechleri): Translating to "Dragon's Blood," this resin is harvested from the tree of the same name. It's known for its antiseptic and wound-healing properties and is often used in protective magic.

- Palo Santo (Bursera graveolens): Although more commonly associated with South American Shamanism, Palo Santo is revered for its spiritually purifying properties. It's often burned as an incense to cleanse spaces and ward off negative energies.

- Chacruna (Psychotria viridis): Usually used in tandem with Ayahuasca, Chacruna leaves contain the powerful psychoactive compound DMT. On its own, Chacruna is used for spiritual purification and to gain visionary insights.

Ethnobotany and Preservation

As we learn from Amazonian plant magic, it's crucial to approach this wisdom with a sense of humility and respect, acknowledging the long history and deeply embedded traditions of indigenous communities. Unfortunately, the commercialization of some Amazonian plants like Ayahuasca has led to overharvesting and cultural appropriation. Therefore, anyone interested in using these plants for spiritual practices must do so responsibly, considering ethical sourcing and sustainability.

One way to encourage the sustainable practice of Amazonian plant magic is by contributing to conservation efforts, respecting indigenous land rights, and advocating for ethnobotanical research. These measures help preserve the biodiversity of the

Amazon and protect the wisdom of its people, who are the original stewards of this mystical botanical world.

Summary

The lush expanse of the Amazon Rainforest is a treasure trove of botanical magic deeply woven into the fabric of indigenous cultures. From Ayahuasca to Palo Santo, the plants of the Amazon offer profound spiritual insights, healing attributes, and magical properties. While these botanicals have much to teach us, they also beckon us to be ethical stewards of the land and traditions from which they spring. With mindfulness and respect, the rich tapestry of Amazonian plant magic can become an invaluable part of one's own spiritual journey.

CHAPTER 19: AFRICAN ROOTS: PLANTS IN TRADITIONAL AFRICAN RELIGIONS

Introduction

As we explore the role of plants in the magical tapestry of human spirituality, Africa presents a treasure trove of fascinating uses, rituals, and belief systems connected to botany. Traditional African religions such as Vodun, Ifá, and others employ an assortment of plants to facilitate connections with the divine, ancestors, and elemental spirits. In this chapter, we'll delve into some of these traditional African religious systems and examine the role plants play in rituals, divination, and spiritual well-being.

Plants in Ifá: The Religion of Divination

Ifá is a system of divination that originated among the Yoruba people in southwestern Nigeria. It is practiced across various African countries and has found its way to the Americas, mainly through the African diaspora. Plants play a significant role in Ifá rituals, and each plant corresponds to a specific Odu or divination sign. The leaves of the kola nut tree, for example, are used in an elaborate ceremony where the diviner, known as Babalawo, throws a set of objects onto a wooden tray to receive messages from Orunmila, the deity of wisdom and divination.

Herbs like Ewe Iyerosun, a special type of camwood, are used for marking the divination tray and drawing figures representing the Odu. Ewe Iyerosun is believed to have the power to make the divine messages clear. The use of these specific plants is not arbitrary; each plant is chosen based on its unique vibrational energies that align with the specific forces being invoked during divination.

Vodun and its Herbal Practices

Vodun, often spelled Voodoo, is another traditional African religion that originated in West Africa, particularly in what is now Ghana, Togo, and Benin. The practice has a rich botanical tradition used for protection, love, and health, among other intentions. For example, the "African basil" or Ocimum gratissimum, known locally as "Efinrin" or "Djèman," is used in rituals to invoke peace and tranquility. Another plant, Calotropis procera, locally called "Asclepias" or "Sodom Apple," is believed to have protective energies and is used in various protective amulets and charms.

These plants are usually gathered following strict rituals, often at particular times such as at midnight or during a specific moon phase, to capture their full magical potency. The botanicals might then be prepared in various forms—dried, grounded, or extracted—to be used in ritual baths, incense, or magical sachets.

Medicinal and Spiritual Convergence in African Herbalism

Traditional African religions often do not draw a hard line between the spiritual and the medicinal. For instance, in Zulu herbal medicine, also known as "Muti," plants like the African potato (Hypoxis hemerocallidea) and the cancer bush (Sutherlandia frutescens) are used both for their medicinal attributes and their supposed magical properties. These herbs might be employed in rituals to remove evil spirits or protect against negative energies but also serve practical roles in treating physical ailments.

Herbalists or "Sangomas" act as both spiritual guides and healers, employing their extensive knowledge of plants to treat both body and soul. This convergence reflects a holistic worldview where spiritual and physical well-being are intrinsically linked, and plants serve as bridges between these realms.

Conclusion

Plants in traditional African religions are more than mere botanical specimens; they are intricate parts of spiritual cosmologies that have evolved over millennia. Whether it's the use of kola nut leaves in Ifá divination, the protective powers of Calotropis procera in Vodun, or the multifaceted applications of herbs in Zulu Muti, each plant serves a unique spiritual function beyond its physical properties. This intricate relationship between plants and spirituality in Africa enriches the global tapestry of magical botany, revealing yet another layer in the complex ways humans interact with the plant kingdom for spiritual growth and insight.

CHAPTER 20:
CREATING MAGICAL
OILS AND TINCTURES

Introduction

Welcome to a realm where the alchemical meets the botanical, and where your kitchen turns into a laboratory of magical possibilities. Crafting your own magical oils and tinctures offers not just a profound connection with the plant kingdom but also the opportunity to imbue these concoctions with your intent. This chapter guides you through the process of creating these potent solutions, presenting the lore, methods, and practices that make them effective in spiritual and magical endeavors.

The Lore Behind Magical Oils and Tinctures

Before diving into how to make your own oils and tinctures, it's valuable to understand the traditional beliefs and principles behind them. In ancient civilizations like Egypt, Mesopotamia, and even among the Druids, oils and tinctures were considered vital tools for connecting with the divine. They were thought to house the essence or spirit of the plant, thereby granting access to its magical properties. This is closely tied to the concept of "sympathetic magic," where like attracts like. By capturing the plant's essence, you not only access its mundane benefits but also its magical attributes.

When talking about oils, we usually refer to "carrier oils," such as olive, jojoba, or almond oil, that are infused with herbs, roots, or flowers. Tinctures, on the other hand, employ alcohol or vinegar to extract the plant's properties. Both methods offer different advantages. Oils are generally more suited for topical application and anointing, while tinctures are versatile enough to be taken internally or added to various potions and recipes.

Methodologies: Crafting Your Oils and Tinctures

Creating magical oils and tinctures is a relatively simple yet highly intentional activity. Here are the general steps for each:

<u>Magical Oils</u>

- Select a carrier oil. Olive oil is often recommended for its longevity and minimal scent.
- Choose your plant material. Research the plant's magical attributes to ensure it aligns with your intent.
- Cleanse and consecrate your plant material and tools.
- Place the plant material in a glass jar, then pour the carrier oil over it.
- Seal the jar and place it in a sunny or warm location for a period, usually around 4-6 weeks, occasionally shaking it.
- Strain out the plant material, and your magical oil is ready for use.

<u>Magical Tinctures</u>

- Select your solvent—usually high-proof alcohol or apple cider vinegar.
- Follow steps 2-3 as you would for magical oils.
- Place the plant material in a glass jar, and cover it with the solvent.
- Seal and store in a cool, dark place, shaking it daily for about 2-4 weeks.
- Strain the liquid, and it's ready for use or further magical workings.

Always remember to label your oils and tinctures with the date of creation and the plants used. You can also say a spell or incantation during any step in these processes to further imbue the mixture with your magical intentions.

The Role of Astrological Timing and Lunar Phases

While optional, many practitioners swear by the efficacy of creating oils and tinctures during specific astrological and lunar phases. For instance, making a love tincture during a Venus transit or crafting a prosperity oil during the waxing moon could add an additional layer of potency. Traditional texts like the "Picatrix" or even modern planetary tables can be consulted for auspicious times to begin these projects.

Conclusion

Creating your own magical oils and tinctures isn't merely a practical endeavor; it's an intimate act of co-creation with the natural world. It allows you to become an alchemist in your own right, mingling the physical and the ethereal into vessels of potent magical energy. The practical knowledge of making oils and tinctures merges seamlessly with the lore and traditions that have been passed down through centuries. These small vials can serve as your personal arsenal in various spiritual practices, whether you're anointing a candle, blessing an amulet, or taking a ritual bath. And with each drop, you'll not only be tapping into the plant's magical attributes but also connecting deeply with the ancient wisdom and mystical synergy of the Earth.

CHAPTER 21: PLANT-BASED TALISMANS AND AMULETS

Introduction

Welcome to another enriching chapter in the labyrinthine world of occult botany! So far, we have delved into the intricate details of plants, from their historical relevance to their magical properties. Now, we take a step further by exploring the use of plants in creating protective and empowering items—talismans and amulets.

The Magical Crafting of Talismans and Amulets

Talismans and amulets are age-old metaphysical tools used for various purposes, from protection against negative influences to attracting good fortune. While talismans are typically crafted to draw something towards you, like love or prosperity, amulets are designed to protect and ward off negative energies. Although the terms are often used interchangeably, their metaphysical roles are slightly different.

Traditionally, metals, stones, and other materials have been used in crafting these magical items, but plants offer a unique vibrational frequency that can be harnessed for similar purposes. The 'spirit' or 'essence' of the plant can be embedded within these items to carry forth its attributes wherever you go.

- Choosing the Right Plant: The first step in crafting a plant-based talisman or amulet is selecting a plant that aligns with your intent. From protective plants like sage and rosemary to love-attracting ones like rose petals, the botanical realm is vast. Research the magical properties of various plants, perhaps even consulting previous chapters of this book, to choose the right one for your needs.
- Preparation and Consecration: Before crafting your item, it is essential to consecrate the plant material. Consecration involves a ritualistic process to cleanse and charge the plant with your intent. This could involve placing the plant under the light of a full moon or invoking elemental energies.
- Crafting Methods: The actual crafting could take various forms. One popular method is to make a sachet or small bag containing the plant material, perhaps along with other magical ingredients. You could also place small plant parts in lockets or use them in layered jar spells.

Combining Plants with Other Elements

Sometimes, a plant's attributes can be significantly amplified when combined with other magical elements like gemstones, metals, or sigils. For instance, if you're creating a love amulet, you might choose to use rose petals along with a piece of rose quartz. Combining plant material with the right elemental property can create a potent magical tool.

When doing so, always consider the elemental affiliations of each component. Water-based plants may harmonize well with moonstone, while fire-oriented herbs like cinnamon could be better paired with a fiery gemstone like carnelian. By understanding these synergies, you make your amulet or talisman more powerful.

Ethical Considerations

While crafting plant-based talismans and amulets can be a fulfilling spiritual practice, it is important to exercise ethical harvesting techniques. Sustainability should be a priority. Always take only what you need, and if possible, opt for plants that are abundant or can be easily regrown. Offer a form of gratitude back to the Earth, perhaps by planting a seed or giving a natural offering, to maintain a harmonious relationship with the botanical realm.

Summary

Creating plant-based talismans and amulets is not only a creative endeavor but also a deeply spiritual one. Through the intentional crafting of these items, you bring the natural world closer, carrying its protective or empowering energies with you in your daily life. By selecting the right plants, combining them thoughtfully with other elements, and being mindful of ethical considerations, you contribute to a tradition of magical crafting that honors the sacredness of the plant kingdom.

CHAPTER 22:
BOTANICALS IN
RITUAL BATHS AND
CLEANSINGS

Introduction

The use of water for ritual purification has been a mainstay of spiritual traditions across the world. When infused with the vibrational qualities of various plants, this simple yet vital element becomes a powerful tool for cleansing and transformation. This chapter delves into how you can incorporate botanicals into ritual baths and other purification practices.

The Sacredness of Water and Plants in Ritual Baths

The intersection of water and plant energy in ritual baths is an alchemy as ancient as the practice of spirituality itself. In various traditions, including Wicca, Hoodoo, and Ayurveda, water symbolizes the cleansing of emotional and psychic residues. Meanwhile, the botanicals used carry specific vibrations that help to reset or elevate spiritual energy.

In Wicca and other neopagan traditions, ritual baths often precede major rituals or sabbats to purify the practitioner. Essential oils of sage, lavender, and rosemary may be added to water for their protective and purifying properties. Similarly, in Hoodoo—an African American folk magic tradition—herbal baths are used for a wide range of purposes, from attracting love to banishing negative energies. Common herbs include hyssop, rue, and agrimony, which are steeped in boiling water before being strained and added to the bath.

Ayurveda, the traditional Hindu system of medicine, places emphasis on the balancing of bodily humors (doshas) for holistic wellness. Ritual baths in this tradition often incorporate plants like turmeric, saffron, and holy basil to balance specific doshas and purify the energy body. The water temperature is often adjusted according to one's dominant dosha—Vata, Pitta, or Kapha —to maximize therapeutic effects.

Botanicals for Various Types of Cleansing

Different botanicals serve different purposes in spiritual cleansing, and it's important to align your choices with your intention.

- For Protection: Plants like sage, bay leaves, and cedar are often employed for their protective energies. Infusing them into your bathwater can serve as a shield against psychic or emotional harm.

- For Emotional Healing: Rose petals, chamomile, and lavender are connected with the heart chakra and emotional well-being. A bath infused with these botanicals can be a potent self-care ritual.

- For Spiritual Upliftment: To elevate your spiritual vibrations, consider botanicals like frankincense, myrrh, and sandalwood. These are often used in religious rites and are said to enhance spiritual communication.

Practical Tips for Preparing Your Botanical Bath

Creating a botanical bath doesn't require an elaborate procedure, but there are some guidelines you might find useful:

- Safety First: Make sure you're not allergic to any plants you intend to use. If you're pregnant, consult a healthcare provider before using certain herbs.

- Setting Intention: Before adding botanicals to your bath, hold them in your hand and set an intention for what you wish to achieve—be it protection, emotional healing, or spiritual upliftment.

- Method of Infusion: You can add essential oils directly to the water, or steep herbs in boiling water separately before adding the strained liquid to your bath.

- Temperature and Timing: The water should be comfortably warm but not hot, and immersing yourself for about 20-30 minutes is generally effective. While in the bath, meditate on your intention, letting go of any negative thoughts or emotions.

Conclusion

Ritual baths serve as a crossroads where the elemental energy of water meets the spiritual vibrations of plants, creating a synergistic effect that cleanses both body and soul. Whether it's for protection, emotional healing, or spiritual upliftment, infusing your baths with carefully chosen botanicals can be a deeply rewarding practice. The next time you draw a bath, consider the magical boost that these green allies can provide, enhancing not just your hygiene but your entire spiritual wellbeing.

CHAPTER 23:
KITCHEN WITCHERY:
EDIBLE MAGIC

Introduction

Welcome to a fascinating chapter where the kitchen becomes your magical sanctuary. Here, we'll explore how culinary herbs and spices can take on potent spiritual meanings, going beyond their roles as mere ingredients in recipes. If you've ever been moved by the aroma of rosemary wafting through the air or felt a sense of peace while sipping chamomile tea, you already have a taste of the deep-rooted connections between culinary plants and magic.

The Kitchen as a Sacred Space

Traditionally, the kitchen has been seen as the heart of the home, a space where families gather, traditions are upheld, and nourishment is created. In many spiritual practices, the process of cooking is often seen as a practical alchemy—an intentional blending of ingredients to create something new. This alchemical perspective is especially prevalent in the world of kitchen witchery, where each culinary activity—from chopping and stirring to baking and brewing—becomes a form of spellwork.

Sacred geometry can also play a role in the layout and design of your kitchen. Elements like the placement of the stove, the organization of your spice rack, or even the choice of cooking utensils can all be informed by ancient wisdom. For instance, the triangle often represents the Holy Trinity in Christian mysticism or the Triple Goddess in Wicca. A kitchen layout resembling a triangle, linking the stove, sink, and refrigerator, can create a harmonious flow of energy conducive to magical workings.

Culinary Herbs and Spices: Nature's Little Wonders

In the realm of culinary herbs and spices, many have been attributed with mystical properties throughout the ages. Consider some of these:

- Rosemary: Often associated with remembrance and fidelity, rosemary can be used to reinforce bonds of love and friendship. In European folklore, it was considered protective against evil spirits.

- Sage: A symbol of wisdom and purification, sage is frequently used in cleansing rituals. It's not just for smudging; adding sage to your dishes can also aid in mental clarity and spiritual cleansing.

- Basil: As a symbol of love and fertility, basil is an excellent addition to any dish intended to invoke these energies. In some cultures, it's even used in love spells or given as a symbol of good luck.

- Cinnamon: Often related to the energies of the sun, cinnamon is commonly used to attract prosperity and success. A sprinkle of cinnamon in your morning coffee or oatmeal can serve as a simple spell for a successful day.

- Turmeric: Known for its bright yellow color, turmeric is often linked to the energy of the sun and is used for purification and energization. In Ayurvedic practices, it's heralded for its balancing and healing properties.

Remember, intention is key in magical practices. As you prepare your dish, focus on the energies you want to invoke. Visualize these energies being stirred into your food as you mix your ingredients.

Ritualizing Mealtime

Just as how you prepare food matters, the act of consuming it can also be ritualized for magical intent. For instance, you could say a brief incantation before eating, infusing your meal with a specific purpose. Even the act of sharing food can be significant; it's an age-old form of creating and deepening bonds.

In some traditions, it's also common to leave offerings of food for spiritual entities, as a sign of respect and gratitude. These can be small portions of the meals you've prepared, placed on a designated altar or offering space. Over time, this practice can strengthen your connection with the spiritual realm, transforming your kitchen into a hub of magical activity.

Conclusion

The magical potential of culinary herbs and spices extends far beyond their delicious flavors and tantalizing aromas. They serve as versatile tools for spiritual transformation right in the heart of your home—the kitchen. By viewing cooking as a form of practical alchemy and ritual, and by using herbs and spices imbued with magical properties, you open the door to a rich tradition that elevates the simple act of making and consuming food to a sacred art. This chapter has given you the groundwork to make your kitchen a magical sanctuary, transforming everyday cooking into a meaningful spiritual practice.

CHAPTER 24: GREEN WITCHCRAFT AND URBAN BOTANY

Introduction

The concrete jungle need not be a place devoid of magic. In fact, urban settings can provide a unique and enriching backdrop for botanical witchcraft. Green witchcraft traditionally conjures images of forested groves and pastoral landscapes, yet the heart of this practice is about connecting with nature wherever it flourishes, even in cityscapes. This chapter explores the exciting possibilities and methods for practicing green witchcraft within urban settings, leveraging city-specific botanical resources for magical use.

Foraging in Urban Landscapes

While it may seem that city life offers limited opportunities for foraging, many urban areas are rife with edible and medicinal plants. Dandelions, clover, chickweed, and nettles often pop up in parks, near roadways, or even through cracks in the pavement. Being aware of your environment is key. It's critical to ensure that the areas you're foraging from aren't contaminated with pesticides, heavy metals, or other pollutants.

When foraging, ethically sourcing plants is pivotal. Only take what you can use, and always make sure to leave enough for the plant to continue growing and for wildlife to use as well. A practice of gratitude toward the plants you collect can be as simple as offering a small token, like a piece of biodegradable thread, or as profound as a whispered thank-you to the plant spirit.

Window Sills and Balconies: Your Mini Magical Garden

Not everyone has access to a garden plot, but many of us have window sills, balconies, or small patios. These can be potent spaces for growing magical plants. Even if your apartment lacks direct sunlight, many plants associated with magical practices thrive in partial shade. Consider growing herbs like mint, basil, or chives, which are not only culinary stars but also carry various magical properties. Mint can be used for prosperity spells, basil for love, and chives for protection.

When planting in limited spaces, vertical gardening can be a great solution. Stackable planters or wall-mounted pockets can hold a variety of herbs and small plants, turning even a tiny balcony into a lush, magical garden. The act of tending to these plants becomes a ritual in itself, one that fosters a connection with the earth even within an urban environment.

The Importance of Local Plant Spirits

One of the beautiful aspects of green witchcraft is the relationship formed with plant spirits. In an urban setting, these relationships can be even more meaningful because city plants have adapted to a very specific and often challenging environment. Connecting with these hardy urban plant spirits can yield magical workings that are intensely focused on survival, resilience, and adaptability.

Spend time with local trees, perhaps those lining the streets or in nearby parks. Each type of tree has its own set of magical correspondences. For example, the oak tree is often associated with strength and endurance, while the willow tree is linked to the moon and emotions. Developing relationships with these trees not only enriches your spiritual practice but also fosters a sense of local eco-spirituality.

Conclusion

The city, with its frenetic energy and towering skyscrapers, might not seem like an ideal place for practicing green witchcraft. But magic is about making the everyday extraordinary and finding the sacred in the mundane. Whether it's foraging responsibly from urban green spaces, creating your magical garden on a window sill, or connecting with the resilient plant spirits of the city, the urban landscape offers unique and enriching experiences for your botanical practice. Navigating the intersection of urban life and green witchcraft allows for the creation of a magical practice that is not only profoundly adaptable but also deeply rooted in your immediate environment.

CHAPTER 25:
FENG SHUI AND
THE PLACEMENT
OF PLANTS

Introduction

Welcome to another verdant chapter in this journey through occult botany. In this chapter, we will explore the intriguing subject of Feng Shui, the ancient Chinese practice of harmonizing spaces, and how it intersects with our botanical pursuits. Whether you're a Feng Shui novice or a seasoned practitioner, understanding the role of plants in this art form can elevate your magical and spiritual work.

The Basics of Feng Shui and the Five Elements

Feng Shui, which translates to "wind-water," aims to create a harmonious flow of energy (Qi) in the environment. One way to achieve this balance is through the Five Elements—Wood, Fire, Earth, Metal, and Water. Each of these elements represents different aspects of energy, and when they are balanced, they encourage positive Qi flow.

Now, plants primarily fall under the Wood element in Feng Shui. Wood energy is considered expansive and growth-oriented, often linked to vitality, flexibility, and kindness. It is no surprise that plants, which are ever-growing and reach towards the light, represent this element. By understanding this elemental classification, you can use plants to boost specific types of energy in your surroundings.

Choosing Plants for Feng Shui Areas

In Feng Shui, the layout of your home is divided into different sectors, often represented by the Bagua map. Each sector corresponds to a specific life area like wealth, relationships, or career. Plants can be placed in these areas to strengthen or balance the energies. Here are some general guidelines:

- Wealth and Prosperity Area: Opt for plants with rounded leaves or plants that are particularly lush. Jade plants and money trees are popular choices.

- Love and Relationships Area: Choose plants with pink or red flowers to symbolize love and passion. Roses and orchids can be good options.

- Career and Life Path Area: Go for plants that grow upright but aren't too spiky, as you want the energy to flow freely but not be aggressive. Lucky bamboo is a classic choice.

- Family and Health Area: Opt for plants that are hardy and require less maintenance, symbolizing strong roots and robust health. ZZ plants or snake plants are often recommended.

- Spiritual Growth and Wisdom Area: In this area, plants that have more ethereal or unique appearances can be suitable. Think of air plants or even ferns that have a more intricate leaf pattern.

Caring for Your Feng Shui Plants

Once you've selected your plants and positioned them according to the Bagua map, your responsibility doesn't end there. In Feng Shui, a plant's health is vital. A sick or dying plant can symbolize stagnant or negative energy. Make sure you are watering your plants as needed, providing them with sufficient light and even wiping the dust off their leaves regularly. Also, be attentive to your plants' needs. If a plant seems to struggle despite your best efforts, consider whether it's located in the appropriate Feng Shui area or if it needs to be replaced.

Summary

By integrating Feng Shui principles into your occult botanical practices, you unlock another layer of spiritual and magical potency. Whether you're trying to boost your wealth, attract love, or simply cultivate a harmonious environment, the mindful placement of plants can be a powerful tool in your arsenal. Through the proper selection and care of plants in different areas of your home or sacred space, you can channel the elemental energies that these plants represent, bringing balance, growth, and positive Qi into your life. Now, that's what we call holistic magic—uniting the art of placement with the power of plants.

CHAPTER 26: MAGICAL GARDENS AND SACRED GROVES

Introduction

As we've delved into the captivating world of magical plants, we've uncovered a rich tapestry of knowledge across various cultures, traditions, and practices. While individual plants hold unique powers and attributes, there is an overarching layer of magic when plants are brought together in a garden or grove. Such spaces not only magnify the energies of the individual plants but also create an ethereal environment conducive to spiritual work. In this chapter, we'll explore how you can cultivate a magical garden or sacred grove as a haven for your own spiritual journey.

Building the Foundation: Intentions and Correspondences

Before a single seed is sown or a young sapling planted, defining your intention for your magical garden or sacred grove is critical. Are you looking to create a space for healing, meditation, ritualistic work, or perhaps a combination of these? Understanding your primary purpose will guide you in selecting the appropriate plants, layout, and even the timeframes for planting and harvesting.

Just as individual plants have their own magical correspondences —linked to elements, celestial bodies, or specific spells—so does the space that will house them. Consider these alignments when laying out your garden. For instance, if your primary focus is healing, plants associated with medicinal properties and lunar energies may be grouped in a corner that receives ample moonlight.

Energetic Blueprint: Geometry and Layout

The design of your garden or grove can significantly influence the flow of energy within the space. Traditional patterns like the labyrinth, mandala, or the Tree of Life from Qabalah can be used as blueprints for your garden. These geometrical figures aren't just aesthetically pleasing; they are time-tested configurations that channel energy in specific ways. For example, a labyrinth can be a path for introspective walking meditations, while a mandala garden could serve as a visual focus for broader cosmic contemplation.

The concept of "Sacred Geometry," often cited in various magical traditions, can also be applied here. Sacred Geometry posits that specific shapes and proportions—like the spiral, the Golden Ratio, or the Vesica Piscis—are inherently powerful and harmonious, mirroring the very structure of the universe. Incorporating these forms into your garden layout can amplify the magical qualities of the space.

Subtle Energies: Elementals and Ley Lines

While most gardens benefit from good soil, adequate water, and proper sunlight, magical gardens and groves can gain an additional layer of potency by aligning with natural concentrations of Earth's energy, often referred to as ley lines. These are invisible channels of Earth's magnetic field, said to crisscross the globe. While the scientific community remains divided on this issue, many practitioners swear by the enhanced vitality and effectiveness of magical workings when conducted on or near a ley line.

Other natural entities, like elementals associated with the four classical elements—earth, water, fire, and air—can be invited to reside in your garden or grove. In some traditions, small elemental altars might be set up to honor these entities, perhaps consisting of a rock formation for Earth, a birdbath or fountain for Water, a ceramic fire pit for Fire, and wind chimes for Air.

Summary

Creating a magical garden or sacred grove is much more than a mere horticultural project; it's a sacred endeavor that marries botany with the realm of the mystical. By paying heed to intentions and correspondences, adopting geometrically and energetically potent layouts, and even aligning with Earth's natural energies, you can establish a space that serves not just as a visual or olfactory delight but as a potent zone for spiritual work. Whether you're a solitary practitioner or part of a community, such gardens and groves can become your sanctuaries, aiding and amplifying your magical practice. From the roots in the Earth to the branches reaching towards the sky, your magical garden will stand as a living testament to the symbiosis between the botanical world and the esoteric one, each nurturing and elevating the other.

CHAPTER 27: PLANTS AND ASTROLOGY: CELESTIAL CORRESPONDENCES

Introduction

Astrology, the study of celestial bodies and their influence on human affairs, has been an integral part of magical practice for centuries. As we delve into the realm of occult botany, it's intriguing to consider how the energies of planets, stars, and astrological signs can be intertwined with the magic of plants. In this chapter, we explore the rich connections between astrology and the botanical world.

The Zodiac and Botanical Correspondences

One of the most captivating intersections of astrology and botany lies in the correspondence between zodiac signs and specific plants. According to various traditions, each zodiac sign is associated with specific herbs, trees, or flowers that are believed to resonate with the particular energy of that sign. For instance:

- Aries, ruled by Mars, is often associated with plants like thistles and nettles that have thorns or prickly leaves, echoing the fiery and assertive nature of the sign.

- Taurus, ruled by Venus, resonates with roses and foxgloves, embodying the sensual and stable nature of the Earth sign.

- Gemini, under Mercury's influence, connects with plants like lavender and dill that are versatile and aid in communication, reflecting the sign's dual nature and love for dialogue.

Understanding these correspondences can help in creating personalized magical spells, rituals, and plant-based remedies that are aligned with your astrological profile.

Planetary Correspondences in Herbalism

Just as zodiac signs have their corresponding plants, so do the planets. These correspondences stem from the ancient belief that the planets ruled certain physical and emotional traits. Consequently, plants were categorized based on the characteristics they shared with these celestial bodies:

- Sun: Plants like sunflowers and calendula, which open

during daylight and are heliotropic (turning toward the sun), are linked to the Sun's energy of vitality and life-force.

- Moon: Plants like jasmine and water lilies, which bloom at night or have a deep connection to water, are attributed to the Moon, representing intuition, dreams, and emotions.

- Saturn: Slow-growing or long-living plants like yew trees and comfrey are associated with Saturn, symbolizing structure, limitations, and the passage of time.

These planetary correspondences can offer profound insights when crafting magical oils, incense, or talismans, as well as when planting or harvesting in tune with celestial cycles.

Astrological Timing in Magical Botany

The influence of celestial bodies isn't limited to correspondences; it also extends to timing. Astrological timing can be crucial when sowing seeds, harvesting herbs, or executing any magical work involving plants. Various phases of the moon, planetary hours, and even specific astrological transits can be leveraged to enhance the potency of your botanical endeavors.

For instance, the New Moon is often considered an ideal time for planting seeds, symbolizing new beginnings and growth. On the other hand, the Full Moon is seen as an opportune time for harvesting, as the plants are believed to be at their peak energy. Such considerations can be incredibly nuanced; even the day of the week can have astrological significance tied to a particular planet, thereby affecting the efficacy of your botanical magic.

Conclusion

Understanding the intricate relationships between astrology and plants opens a new dimension in the practice of occult botany. It offers a nuanced approach, letting you harmonize the energies of celestial bodies with your botanical magic for more effective and personalized rituals. Whether you're matching zodiac signs with their corresponding herbs or timing your garden activities according to lunar phases, the marriage between astrology and botany offers an enriching layer to your magical and spiritual journey.

CHAPTER 28:
CULTIVATING RARE
MAGICAL PLANTS

Introduction

In the lush tapestry of the magical botanical world, there are many common plants that most people have heard of, like sage for cleansing or lavender for calming. However, as we venture further into the realms of occult botany, we come across rarer, more esoteric species that carry unique magical properties. In this chapter, we will focus on the cultivation of these rare magical plants, some of which are often elusive due to their specific growing conditions or geographic locales.

Challenges in Cultivating Rare Plants

Rare magical plants come with their set of challenges, both practical and ethical. From a practical standpoint, many rare plants have specific soil, climate, and watering needs. If you're aiming to cultivate a desert plant like white sage (Salvia apiana) in a temperate region, you'll need to simulate the plant's native conditions as closely as possible, perhaps by using specialized planters or greenhouses. Additionally, some of these plants may require a longer growing season than is naturally available in your area.

Ethically, there's a fine line between cultivation for personal use and contributing to the endangerment of a species. Overharvesting is a concern with many rare plants, so it's crucial to understand sustainable harvesting methods and, where possible, to propagate your plants to aid in their conservation. Ensure that any seeds or cuttings are sourced responsibly, ideally from certified suppliers who engage in sustainable practices.

Techniques for Growing Rare Plants

Several techniques can be employed to grow these mystical botanical wonders:

- Microclimate Creation: Use of barriers like windbreaks, or creating sun-traps can help you simulate the plant's natural habitat.

- Soil Amendment: Research the specific soil chemistry preferred by the plant. You may need to add particular nutrients or adjust the pH level.

- Light Cycles: Some rare plants are sensitive to the duration and intensity of light. Indoor grow lights with timers can help control these conditions.

- Watering Regimens: While some magical plants, like the water-loving willow (Salix spp.), prefer constant moisture, others like the aforementioned white sage require periods of dryness.

Preservation through Propagation

As someone involved in the practice of magical botany, you are also a steward of these mystical beings. Many rare plants can be propagated through cuttings, seed collection, or even root division. This not only ensures that you have a continuous supply for your magical work but also plays a part in the preservation of the species. Ensure that you follow the best practices for each propagation method and consider sharing your plants with like-minded individuals to further their distribution.

If you have successfully propagated a rare plant, consider participating in seed exchange programs or donating some specimens to botanical gardens focused on conservation. This helps to preserve the genetic diversity of the plant, ensuring its longevity and resilience for future generations.

Summary

The cultivation of rare magical plants offers the chance to delve deeper into the esoteric aspects of botanical magic, providing you with unique energies and attributes to enhance your practice. While growing these plants can be challenging, the rewards, both magical and ethical, make the endeavor deeply fulfilling. By cultivating these plants, you contribute to a lineage of magical and conservation practices that honor the richness of Earth's biodiversity.

Remember, each plant you nurture becomes part of your own magical ecosystem, a living embodiment of the mysteries that you hold dear. Through mindful cultivation and responsible propagation, you become not just a practitioner but a guardian of the Earth's rare and magical flora.

CHAPTER 29:
GEOMANCY AND
PLANT MAGIC

Introduction

As we journey deeper into the green mysteries of occult botany, we stumble upon geomancy—a divinatory art that interacts profoundly with the earth. In this chapter, we'll explore the synergistic relationship between geomancy and plant magic, learning how these two ancient practices can complement and enhance each other in various spiritual contexts.

The Fundamentals of Geomancy

Geomancy, meaning 'divining the Earth,' is an age-old method of divination that interprets markings on the ground or patterns formed by tossing soil, rocks, or sand. The practice has its roots in various cultural traditions including Arabic, African, and European systems of esoteric wisdom. It involves the creation of sixteen figures or patterns, each with its own meaning and associations, that are then interpreted to answer questions or gain insight into a situation.

In the Western esoteric tradition, geomantic figures are often correlated with astrological signs, elements, and even planets, offering a comprehensive system for understanding the cosmos and one's place in it. As a practice intimately connected with the Earth, it's not surprising that geomancy has many touchpoints with the world of plants.

Plants as Geomantic Tools

Plants can serve as potent instruments in geomantic rituals and practices. Here are a few ways they can be integrated:

- Plant Markers for Geomantic Figures: Certain plants can be used to create the actual geomantic figures on the ground. For example, a practitioner might use willow twigs to form the figures, given willow's associations with intuition and emotional insight. This would add another layer of meaning to the geomantic process.

- Herbal Infusions for Grounding: Prior to engaging in geomantic divination, a practitioner could consume an herbal tea made from grounding plants like mugwort or valerian root to enhance their connection to Earth energies.

- Incenses and Resins: Burning plant-based incenses can

facilitate a more intuitive and connected geomantic reading. Frankincense, for instance, can clear the space and enhance concentration, while sage can purify the area where the geomancy is taking place.

- Creating Plant-based Geomantic Sigils: Drawing geomantic figures with plant-based inks can infuse the practice with specific plant energies. Oak gall ink, for example, which is traditionally made from oak galls and iron salts, carries the steadfast and durable qualities of the oak tree, thereby influencing the geomantic reading accordingly.

Geomancy in Magical Gardens and Sacred Groves

A magical garden or a sacred grove can serve as a living geomantic chart where plants represent geomantic figures or elements. Designing such a space involves a thoughtful selection of plants that not only correspond to geomantic symbolism but also grow harmoniously together. Here, both the practical aspects of botany and the mystical elements of geomancy can guide the planting process. For example, an area of the garden might be dedicated to plants associated with the geomantic figure 'Amissio,' which relates to loss and letting go. Plants like rue or wormwood, often linked to purification and banishing rituals, could be appropriate choices.

This kind of spiritually-infused permaculture allows for an environment where both plants and geomantic energies can thrive symbiotically. The garden becomes a living oracle, a place where one can seek spiritual guidance and healing. By walking through it, the practitioner interacts directly with the geomantic figures, receiving wisdom not just through intellectual understanding but through bodily experience and communion with the plants.

Summary

Geomancy and plant magic are two venerable traditions that can enrich one another in numerous ways. Whether by using plants as tools and markers in geomantic divination, incorporating them into geomantically-informed magical gardens, or using plant-based products like incenses and teas to enhance geomantic practices, these two realms offer opportunities for deepening our connection to the Earth and its many layers of meaning. Indeed, when geomancy and plant magic are combined, the resulting practice becomes a powerful synthesis of wisdom that speaks directly to the soul, rooted deeply in the Earth yet infinitely expansive.

CHAPTER 30: PLANTS IN HEALING AND DIVINATION

Introduction

In the grand tapestry of magical botany, plants play versatile roles that transcend mere aesthetic or culinary applications. They can serve as our allies in spiritual, emotional, and physical healing, as well as tools in divination—the art of gaining insights or foretelling events. In this chapter, we will delve into the ways that plants can be used in both healing practices and divination methods across various spiritual traditions.

The Healing Aspect of Plants

The idea of plants possessing healing properties is as old as human civilization itself. Ancient Egyptian papyrus scrolls refer to herbal remedies, and Ayurvedic texts from India lay down the uses of plants like turmeric and holy basil for wellness. Western traditions also have their fair share, such as the Doctrine of Signatures, which suggests that the appearance of a plant may indicate its healing attributes.

Yet, the healing we refer to here extends beyond the physical and ventures into the metaphysical realm. In many pagan and animistic traditions, plants are believed to contain specific energies or vibrations. For example, lavender is not just good for physical relaxation but is also considered a plant of love, peace, and mental clarity in magical workings. These spiritual attributes can be harnessed through various methods like brewing teas, creating sachets, or even meditative contemplation of a plant's form and texture.

Practitioners often place healing plants on altars, use them to circle a ritual space, or carry them as talismans. The concept is that the plant's energy can interact with human energy fields to bring about needed changes. The practice relies on a deep, respectful relationship with the plant, including acknowledging the spirit or essence of the plant. Some may opt to communicate with this essence through prayer, asking for its assistance in healing.

Divinatory Practices Involving Plants

Divination, another ancient practice, utilizes various tools and techniques to gain wisdom or knowledge that isn't readily available to the rational mind. Plants can be employed in divination practices in intriguing ways. Let's explore a few:

- Pythia Botanomancy: This form of divination involves throwing plant matter into a fire and interpreting the flames, smoke, or the sound the plants make as they burn. Sage, cedar, and mugwort are popular choices for their potent energetic signatures and distinct behaviors when burned.

- Alectryomancy with Grains: While not strictly plant-based, this form of divination involves scattering grains or seeds (often barley) and observing the patterns in which they fall or are picked by birds. This method is derived from practices in ancient Rome and Greece.

- Dendromancy: This is the art of divination using trees. It can involve interpreting the natural patterns found on bark, the way leaves fall, or even the general health and aura of the tree.

- Haruspication with Herbs: Inspired by a form of divination from ancient Mesopotamia, this method involves inspecting the entrails of sacrificed animals. However, a less gruesome and more modern version uses herbs. The herbs are steeped in water, and the resulting shapes and patterns of the leaves are interpreted.

Each of these methods has its roots in longstanding traditions, and while they may appear arcane, they are being used today by modern practitioners who find value in these ancient arts.

Ethical and Practical Considerations

When engaging with plants in these spiritual ways, ethics should be a fundamental concern. Always source your plants sustainably and respectfully. Acknowledge the life and energy of the plant, and if you are harvesting it yourself, do so in a way that allows the plant to continue to thrive. Ensure that you're using plants that are not endangered and be cautious to identify plants accurately, especially if you're using them in a way that involves ingestion or skin contact.

Conclusion

The applications of plants in healing and divination are rich and varied, grounded in ancient traditions yet adaptable to modern practices. As we engage with the mystical energies of plants, we tap into a form of ancestral wisdom that has been passed down through generations. The key is to approach this practice with respect, both for the plants themselves and for the traditions from which these practices originate. In doing so, you not only enrich your own spiritual journey but also contribute to the vast, interconnected web of life that sustains us all.

CHAPTER 31:
THE ETHICS OF
PLANT MAGIC

Introduction

As we delve into the magical properties and uses of plants, it becomes essential to address an often-overlooked facet: the ethics of plant magic. Engaging with plant magic is more than just reading spells and collecting herbs; it involves understanding the deeper implications of our actions on both spiritual and ecological levels.

Ethical Harvesting

One of the primary ethical concerns in plant magic is the method and manner in which plant materials are harvested. Here, the doctrine of sustainable harvesting takes center stage. When harvesting wild plants, it's important to consider the plant's population, season, and role in its ecosystem. In some cases, the roots are the part used in magical practices, and taking the roots kills the plant. Therefore, unless the plant is abundant and its removal will not adversely affect the local ecology, it's best to look for alternatives.

Sustainable harvesting also means ensuring that you're not endangering plants that are already at risk of extinction. Overharvesting has led to the decline of various plant species, some of which hold immense magical significance. For example, American Ginseng, which is used in various magical and medicinal practices, has been listed as an endangered species due to overharvesting. Practitioners should always look for ethically sourced materials, perhaps even considering cultivated alternatives to wild-harvested plants.

The Ethical Use of Plant Materials

The ethical dimension extends to how we use the plant materials we collect. Using plants for nefarious purposes not only conflicts with many ethical paradigms but also is believed by many traditions to bring negative karma or other undesirable consequences. The intent matters in magical practices; hence, the use of plant magic for manipulative or harmful goals often contradicts ethical guidelines in most spiritual paths.

Another issue is the use of plants with strong psychoactive effects, like certain types of mushrooms or the peyote cactus. These plants are often integral to specific spiritual traditions and rituals. Their use outside of these contexts can be seen as culturally insensitive or appropriative, not to mention potentially illegal in some jurisdictions.

Fair Trade and Economic Ethics

The rise in popularity of plant magic has led to an increase in demand for exotic herbs, resins, and other plant materials. Unfortunately, this has occasionally resulted in unethical harvesting and trade practices, including exploitative labor conditions. Practitioners should strive to source their materials from suppliers who are certified as engaging in fair trade. This ensures that those involved in the harvesting and initial production phases are paid fairly and work in humane conditions.

Purchasing from local growers or cultivating your own magical herbs can also reduce your ecological footprint. Shipping herbs across large distances involves significant energy expenditure and contributes to your overall carbon footprint. Local or homegrown herbs are not only fresher but also more ecologically responsible.

Conclusion

Incorporating ethics into your magical practice may require extra effort in terms of research and sourcing, but it enriches your practice by aligning it with the cycles and balance of nature, which is often the source of the magic to begin with. Just as you are drawing on the plants for spiritual nourishment and support, so too should you aim to nourish and support the plants and the ecosystems they belong to. Remember, ethical considerations are not just add-ons but are integral to a deep, meaningful, and sustainable magical practice.

By adopting a more ethical approach, you affirm the interconnectedness of all life and contribute to a more harmonious relationship between the human and the botanical realms. Plant magic then becomes not just a set of techniques for personal transformation, but a path that transforms the world around you, one ethical choice at a time.

CHAPTER 32: TECHNO-BOTANY: DIGITAL AND VIRTUAL PLANTS

Introduction

As we navigate the digital age, the boundaries between the natural world and the digital realm are becoming increasingly blurred. Technological advancements have ushered in new modes of engagement with traditional occult practices, including the realm of magical botany. This chapter delves into the emerging field of techno-botany, exploring how digital and virtual plants are finding their way into contemporary magical practices.

Virtual Gardens: Simulated Spaces with Real Intent

With advancements in Virtual Reality (VR) and Augmented Reality (AR), a new frontier has opened up for practitioners of plant-based magic. These technologies allow for the creation of simulated natural environments that can be as vivid and interactive as physical ones. In these virtual gardens, users can grow, tend, and interact with a variety of digital plants that possess qualities similar to their real-world counterparts.

Does cultivating a digital plant have the same magical impact as nurturing a physical one? The jury is still out, but some practitioners argue that intentionality plays a significant role. For example, the same principles used to imbue a physical plant with magical intention can be applied in a virtual setting. While VR and AR plants may not produce physical essential oils or incense, they can serve as potent symbols or astral counterparts, and may be especially useful for those who don't have the space or capability to cultivate a physical garden.

Digital Alchemy: Encoding Spells and Intentions

In traditional plant magic, practitioners might create an herbal sachet or talisman with specific intentions or perform a ritual to imbue a plant with a magical purpose. In the digital realm, this can be translated into programming and encoding. Digital alchemists work with lines of code as they would with stems and roots, weaving intentionality into the very architecture of a virtual plant.

For instance, imagine a piece of software designed to simulate the growth of a digital 'sage' plant, known traditionally for its cleansing properties. The practitioner could code specific algorithms that correlate with phases of the moon, or other celestial events, for optimal "growth" and potency. When the virtual sage is "burned" within the simulation, the act triggers a ripple in the encoded data, culminating in a digital cleansing effect. While it may not replace the sensory experience of smelling real sage, the symbolic act can still be a powerful means of aligning one's intentions with the digital act.

Ethical Considerations in Techno-Botany

As with any form of magical practice, techno-botany comes with its own set of ethical considerations. Digital plants, unlike their organic counterparts, do not possess inherent life forces or a physical connection to the Earth. However, they do consume energy in the form of electricity and computing power. As practitioners, it's crucial to recognize and minimize the environmental impact of our digital activities.

Moreover, if you're using a platform or software created by others, remember to respect intellectual property rights. Just as you wouldn't pluck a rare plant from someone else's garden without permission, you should not appropriate or tamper with someone else's digital creation without consent.

Conclusion

While the emerging realm of techno-botany is exciting, it raises complex questions around efficacy, ethics, and environmental responsibility. Virtual and digital plants can serve as extensions or complements to physical practices, offering innovative ways to engage with ancient traditions in a modern context. As with all magical practices, the key lies in balance—integrating new methodologies while preserving the essence of time-honored wisdom. As technology continues to advance, it will be fascinating to see how digital landscapes further intertwine with the magical lore of plants, opening up uncharted territories in the quest for spiritual enlightenment.

CHAPTER 33: PLANTS IN MODERN PAGAN FESTIVALS

Introduction

In this journey through the esoteric botanical world, we've covered everything from historical roots and ethics to the merging of plants and technology. Now, let's take a moment to appreciate the role plants play in modern Pagan celebrations. Although modern Paganism draws inspiration from ancient traditions, it is very much a living, evolving practice that integrates plants in a variety of meaningful ways.

The Wheel of the Year and Seasonal Plants

One of the foundational aspects of modern Paganism is the observance of the Wheel of the Year, a cycle of eight seasonal festivals including the solstices, equinoxes, and cross-quarter days. Each of these festivals, such as Imbolc, Beltane, Lammas, and Samhain, has specific plants associated with them that serve both symbolic and practical purposes.

For example, during Beltane, hawthorn is often used in

celebrations. Hawthorn branches are hung on doors and windows to bring blessings and fertility. In the festival of Samhain, pumpkins and gourds take center stage. They are carved and illuminated to represent the spirit world and the thinning of the veil between realms. The Yule celebration during the Winter Solstice incorporates evergreen trees, holly, and mistletoe as symbols of eternal life and the return of the sun. The use of specific plants during these festivals not only resonates with the energy of the season but also offers a tactile, sensory-rich dimension to celebrations.

Plants as Offerings and Ritual Components

Beyond seasonal festivals, modern Pagan practices often incorporate plants as offerings to deities, spirits, or ancestors. In many rituals and spells, plant elements such as leaves, fruits, and roots are used for their magical properties. For instance, sage, lavender, and rosemary may be burned as incense during rituals for purification. In Wiccan rites, a wand made from willow or yew might be employed as a magical tool for directing energy.

Plant-based offerings are usually chosen based on their correspondences with specific deities or intents. For example, an offering to Aphrodite might include roses, while an offering to Cernunnos, the horned god of Celtic tradition, might include grains or fruits of the season. The thoughtfulness that goes into selecting the right plant amplifies the practitioner's intent, making the ritual or offering that much more powerful.

Plants in Pagan Crafts and Talismans

Another interesting aspect is the making of craft items and

talismans from plants. Whether it's crafting a wand from a specific type of wood, braiding a crown of flowers for a festival, or creating a talismanic pouch filled with selected herbs, modern Pagans make extensive use of plants in their crafts. These crafts serve not just aesthetic purposes but also carry the magical attributes of the plants from which they are made.

Creating these items usually involves a ritualistic approach, from selecting the plant under specific lunar phases to chanting incantations while crafting. For example, a talisman for love might be filled with rose petals, lavender, and apple slices, each selected for their specific magical properties related to love and attraction. When crafted mindfully, these items become potent tools that hold and radiate the magical intentions with which they were created.

Conclusion

Plants continue to play a vital role in modern Pagan practices. They serve as bridges between the spiritual realm and the earthly plane, connecting us through the senses to the cycles and energies of the natural world. From seasonal celebrations to everyday rituals, from offerings to crafts, plants enrich the tapestry of contemporary Pagan life. Their presence in these practices serves as a reminder that while our spiritual paths may evolve, our roots remain deeply connected to the Earth and the bounty it provides.

CHAPTER 34: RARE MANUSCRIPTS AND ANCIENT TEXTS ON PLANT MAGIC

Introduction

As we journey deeper into the world of occult botany, the value of historical insight cannot be underestimated. In this chapter, we will delve into the fascinating realm of rare manuscripts and ancient texts that have discussed the magical properties of plants. These precious documents offer us a window into the minds of our magical ancestors, showcasing how their wisdom and practices have shaped the modern understanding of occult botany.

The Hermetic Corpus and Neoplatonism

One of the foundational texts that explore the relationship between the metaphysical world and plants is the Hermetic Corpus, attributed to Hermes Trismegistus. These texts, originating from Hellenistic Egypt, represent a fusion of Egyptian and Greek thought. Within the Hermetic Corpus, the natural world is seen as a reflection of the divine, and plants occupy a significant place in this schema. The Corpus emphasizes the correspondences between the macrocosm (the universe) and the microcosm (the individual), and plants are considered conduits of divine energy that can help achieve spiritual transformation.

Following this line of thought, Neoplatonists like Plotinus and Proclus also touched upon the spiritual significance of plants. They viewed the natural world, including plants, as emanations from "The One," a formless, ineffable source. For these thinkers, the practice of magic was an intuitive science aimed at aligning one's soul with the divine order, and plants were important tools in this quest.

Medieval Grimoires and Alchemical Texts

During the medieval period, various grimoires (magic books) were authored that featured plant lore prominently. One of the most influential is the "Picatrix," an Arabic work on astrology and magic, which was later translated into Latin. This book contained a plethora of recipes and spells that made extensive use of herbs and other botanical elements for magical workings. From love potions to alchemical concoctions, the Picatrix presented plants as indispensable instruments for both practical and esoteric magic.

Another significant text is the "Book of Abramelin," which details the process of achieving Knowledge and Conversation with one's Holy Guardian Angel. The text includes the usage of specific plant-based oils and incenses as part of its complex magical operation. These medieval texts often borrowed from earlier traditions but added layers of Christian symbolism and ritual structure, creating a synthesis that has influenced Western esotericism for centuries.

In the realm of alchemy, texts like the "Turba Philosophorum" and the works of Paracelsus also discuss the use of plants. For alchemists, plants were not only materials to be used in experiments but also symbols representing various alchemical processes. The transformation of plants, from seed to flower to fruit, mirrored the alchemist's quest for spiritual purification and enlightenment.

Eastern Traditions and Texts

When we turn our gaze toward the East, we find an equally rich tradition of texts concerning the magical properties of plants. In Chinese Taoist literature, like the Daozang, herbs and plants are often discussed for their spiritual and alchemical properties. Certain plants like the lingzhi mushroom are considered to possess life-extending attributes and are incorporated into rituals aimed at immortality.

In the Indian subcontinent, the Atharva Veda, one of the four ancient Vedas, includes hymns and spells that require the use of plants. The text identifies specific botanicals that can ward off evil spirits, heal diseases, and attract prosperity. These plant-based practices were absorbed into later traditions like Ayurveda and Tantra, both of which have their own extensive literature on the magical use of plants.

Conclusion

The exploration of rare manuscripts and ancient texts reveals the ubiquity and diversity of plant lore in magical traditions across time and space. Whether it's the mystical philosophy of the Hermeticists, the practical spells of medieval grimoires, or the life-enhancing practices in Eastern traditions, these texts form an intricate tapestry of knowledge. Understanding these foundational works allows us to appreciate the depth of wisdom that has been passed down through generations. As you continue your journey in occult botany, these texts can serve as invaluable guides, enriching both your intellectual grasp and your practical applications of this ancient yet ever-evolving field.

CHAPTER 35: CONCLUSION: THE LIVING LEGACY OF MAGICAL BOTANY

Introduction

As we stand on the threshold between the mysteries of the past and the possibilities of the future, it's heartening to realize that the magical world of plants remains as compelling as ever. The symbiosis between humans and plants, nourished through centuries of shared history, folklore, and mystical practices, forms a rich tapestry that continues to capture our imagination.

The Continuity of Knowledge

Despite leaps in technology and scientific understanding, the ancient knowledge surrounding the magical attributes of plants holds its ground. The wisdom passed down from our ancestors, scholars, shamans, and herbalists remains relevant, particularly in spiritual and magical practices. In fact, it's not uncommon for modern scientific discoveries to affirm the properties and uses of plants that traditional systems have recognized for ages. Take, for instance, how Ayurveda has used Tulsi (Holy Basil) for thousands of years; modern science now confirms its adaptogenic properties. This harmony between old and new deepens our relationship with the plant kingdom and enriches our magical practices.

Dynamic Evolutions in Practices

As the wheel of time turns, the ways in which we interact with plants in a magical context also evolve. Technological advancements have led to the concept of "Techno-Botany," where digital and virtual plants have a role in contemporary magical practices. Likewise, as ecological concerns loom large, sustainable and ethical approaches to plant magic have become increasingly important. The burgeoning interest in urban botany and the ingenuity with which people adapt their practices to limited spaces further attests to the resilience and adaptability of occult botany.

While the tools and platforms might change, the essential principles—those of connection, transformation, and empowerment—remain consistent. This dynamic nature of magical botany makes it a living legacy, not just a relic of the past.

The Future Is Rooted in the Past

As more people become interested in spiritual practices and alternative modes of healing, the role of magical plants is likely to become increasingly mainstream. Courses, workshops, and even academic studies are making these ancient practices more accessible to a broader audience. As this happens, the custodians of traditional wisdom—the indigenous communities, the spiritual leaders, and practitioners of yore—must not be forgotten. Their contribution in preserving this knowledge is invaluable, and crediting them is not just an ethical necessity but also a means to ensure the authenticity and potency of practices.

Even as new pages are added to the book of occult botany, the roots always trace back to the ancients. In other words, our future discoveries and advancements in the field of magical plants will always be rooted in the wisdom of the past. It is this dialogue between the old and the new that makes the realm of magical botany a fertile ground for endless exploration and growth.

Summary

In the grand scheme of things, plants are not just passive elements of our environment; they are active participants in our physical, emotional, and spiritual well-being. From their roles in ancient myths and rites to their place in modern magical practices, their relevance remains undiminished. The enduring allure of magical botany is not just in its historical depth but also in its future potential. It remains a continuously evolving field, ripe for exploration and rich in opportunities for personal and communal growth. As you close this book, may the seeds of knowledge you've gathered sprout into practice, and may your journey through the magical world of plants be evergreen.

THE END

Printed in Great Britain
by Amazon